The Wonders She Performs

Louis Kaczmarek

Trinity Communications
9380 C1 Forestwood Lane
Manassas, Virginia 22110

DEDICATION

To the Queen of Peace, Our Lady of Fatima;
and to the people of protests
as well as the men of arms,
who in the depths of their souls
truly long for peace with justice.

Table of Contents

ACKNOWLEDGMENTS

I wish to thank Edward J. Moran for his interminable hours of labor, Dr. John Shea for his financial assistance, and Mary McCarthy and Kathryn Lucas, without whose help this book in honor of Our Lady would not have been possible. A special thanks to Patricia Quintiliani for typing the manuscript.

Foreword

You are about to read a book that took ten years to write. In reality, it had its beginnings in 1916 with the three apparitions of the Angel, which prepared the way for the coming of God's Mother at Fatima in 1917. That message from heaven has continued to reach the world through the simple medium of the International Pilgrim Virgin Statue, traveling from diocese to diocese, from country to country. You are about to discover some of the more interesting activities of the Mother of God as she draws millions to her Immaculate Heart so as to present them to her divine Son, saying, "Do whatever he tells you." (John 2:5)

Louis Kaczmarek offers us ten years of his experience as escort of the International Pilgrim Virgin of Fatima. Others have had the task before him. Always the accounts associated with this apostolate have revealed unusual workings of grace through the intercession of the Mother of God. I personally encouraged Louis to accept the opportunity to be the escort of this exceptional sacramental. I knew the ability Louis had as a speaker, his great love for God's Mother. I knew as well his personal efforts at living the spiritual life.

It would be essential that one associated with the marvels of grace frequently occasioned by the visitation of the International Pilgrim Virgin Statue be prepared to struggle with the onslaughts of Satan. Being escort of the International Pilgrim Virgin Statue would involve personal dangers to one's own soul, while it afforded opportunities for grace to millions. A reading of these pages will inform you in some manner of that fact.

When Louis Kaczmarek phoned me that day, over ten years ago, asking whether I thought he should accept the opportunity to be the escort, or work with another apostolate for God's Mother opening up for him, I immediately answered: "Go with the International Pilgrim Virgin Statue. You will be speaking to hundreds of thousands. . . ."

After ten years it is doubtful that there is any living Catholic lay-person in the United States who has preached directly to more souls on a spiritual subject than Louis. More than once Louis has escorted the image of God's Mother around the world, the Image greatly feared by those opposed to the freedom of religion.

At Fatima Our Lady promised, "But in the end, my Immaculate Heart will triumph." I invite you to read these pages and discover how, gradually but definitely, the triumph of Mary's Immaculate Heart is overtaking the world so as to usher in the social reign of Jesus Christ, The King.

Mary is the Queen of Angels. A great battle between the good Angels and the angels of wickedness is being fought on the face of the earth. The spoils of this battle is man, you and me. It is over us they struggle. To the serpent God has said, "I will make you enemies of each other; you and the woman, your offspring and her offspring. . . " (Genesis 3:15). We who are the children of Mary are in battle with the offspring of the serpent. But we have the consolation of both Sacred Scripture and the message of Fatima. The head of the serpent will be crushed and the Woman will triumph.

Read these pages with faith and determination that you will always be a child of Mary.

Father Robert J. Fox
National Spiritual Director
Fatima Youth Apostolate

Introduction

Why is it necessary to have a world wide apostolate of Fatima? Why is it so urgent to travel with the image of the Mother of God from place to place, day in and day out, bringing the message of prayer and penance? In order to understand, it is necessary to have a panoramic view of world history, seen in the light of Revelation. Against that backdrop, it will be easier to grasp the significance of "the wonders She performs."

Mary's shadow falls across all of history. In the book of *Genesis*, the first book of the Bible, God spoke of Mary. After God created Adam and Eve, God's adversary, Satan, persuaded Eve to disobey God; she, in turn, persuaded Adam to repeat her disobedience. God said to Satan, "I will put enmity between you and the woman, and between your offspring and hers" (Genesis 3:15).

From the beginning the battle lines were drawn. On the one side, Mary and her offspring, on the other, Satan and his. The entire history of the world can only be properly understood in the light of the history of Redemption: the Creation, the Fall, the Redemption by the death and resurrection of Jesus, the age of the Church, and the final victory of Christ at the Second Coming and Last Judgement.

Sin cracked God's creation, and the reverberations have sounded and echoed down the long corridors of time. As the centuries passed, the Jewish people waited for the Redeemer with limitless longing. As Isaiah prophesied seven centuries before the birth of Christ, "Therefore the Lord himself will give you this sign: the virgin shall be with child, and bear a Son, and shall name him Immanuel" (Isaiah 7:14).

Anticipating the redemptive merits of Christ, God arranged for the conception of Mary to be without the corruption of original sin—an "advance loan" of grace. In this way, the mother of the Messiah, the mother of the God made flesh, would be the spotless one, the new Eve. Later her son would pay in full for all the sins of the world, and his own mother's exemption from the effects of sin.

In the fullness of time, Isaiah's prophecy came to fruition. Luke tells of the angel Gabriel sent from God to bear stupendous tidings to a virgin of Nazareth named Mary. She is to become the mother of the Messiah by the power of the Holy Spirit. Mary consents, and the Word is made flesh (Luke 1: 26-38).

When Mary's days were accomplished, she bore our Redeemer, and the morning stars sang together for the great day of the new creation—God among us, the Incarnation.

Mary's ministry of intercession is introduced at the wedding feast at Cana;

> At a certain point the wine ran out, and Jesus' mother told him, "They have no more wine." Jesus replied, "Woman, how does this concern of yours involve me? My hour is not yet come." (John 2: 3-4)

By her concern for these needs, Mary had started her role as intercessor which would continue until the end of time.

When Jesus was dying on the cross, He looked down in His agony to His beloved sorrowing mother and His best-loved disciple John: " 'Woman, there is your son.' In turn he said to the disciple, 'There is your mother' " (John 19:26).

The dying Christ calls His mother "woman"—referring to the woman of Genesis. Whereas Eve failed, and her sin is visited upon us, Mary, the perfect pearl of God's creation, succeeded, and through Christ, her Son, became the mother of believers, the mother of the Church.

The "woman" of the Cross is Mother of all believers and Mediatrix of all grace. St. Pius X in "Ad Diem Illum" wrote:

> Hence, Mary, carrying the Savior within her, may be said to have also carried all those whose life was contained in the life of the Savior. Therefore, all of us who are united to Christ and, as the apostle says, "members of His body, of His flesh, and of His bones" [Eph. 5:30] have issued from the womb of Mary like a body joined to its head. Thus, in a spiritual and mystical fashion, we are all children of Mary, and she is Mother of us all. . . .

The enmity between the "woman" and Satan continues to the last days. St. John relates this truth in his prophecies of things that will be in the Church, particularly towards the end of the world in the time of the anti-Christ:

> A great sign appeared in the sky, a woman clothed with the sun, with the moon under her feet, and on her head a crown of twelve stars. . . . Enraged at her escape, the dragon went off to make war on the rest of her offspring, on those who keep God's commandments and give witness to Jesus. (Revelation 12: 1, 17)

In Mexico, in 1531, Mary reminded man that she is the woman of Genesis. The Holy Virgin Mother appeared to the uncle of Juan Diego—Juan Bernardino—and cured him of a fatal illness. She identified herself with the Nahuatl word, "Coatlaxopeuh" meaning, "she who crushes the serpent".[1] The Aztecs were rescued from their brutal paganism; by 1539 eight million were baptized. In a centuries old song, the descendants of the Aztecs praise Mary: "she freed us from great evil; she crushed the serpent's head."

Modern man has cut himself off from his nurturing mother. He has gone out from his Father's house—out into the desert wilderness where the Evil One awaits him. The Mother of God searches him out to save him. In this century, she chose three illiterate peasant children to help her. The world ignores the message Mary brought to Fatima at its peril.

In the year 1916, while the great war raged across Europe, an angel of the Lord came to the green fields of the Cova de Iria, two miles from Fatima, Portugal. There he found the children—Jacinta Marto, a little girl of six; Francisco, her brother, age eight; and their cousin, Lucia dos Santos, age nine. Schooled by conscientious parents, they knew their prayers and catechism; Lucia had made her First Communion. The angel visited the children three times, deepening the children's faith, increasing their love of God, and enlivening their prayer life. He told them they must pray and sacrifice in reparation for the sins of men which offended God, and for the conversion of sinners. On his third visit he brought to all of them the sacrament of the Holy Eucharist. The angel's role appeared to be to prepare the three little children to meet the Mother of God.

The next year, on May 13, Mary appeared. She was announced by lightning in the east; brighter than the sun was the light that surrounded her. The children were terrified. She calmed their fears and asked them to return on the 13th day of the month, at the same time for the next five months. They consented to accepting all the suffering which God would choose to send them, and to offer it in reparation for sin and the conversion of sinners. Mary told them to pray the Rosary daily, and ascended slowly eastward until she vanished in the heavens.

When the children returned the next month, some fifty people accompanied them. Mary predicted the early deaths of Jacinta and Francisco. She again told them to pray the rosary.

In July, the crowd numbered four thousand. As they prayed the Rosary, lightning in the east again announced her arrival. Mary revealed to the three little shepherds a vision of hell, where sinners go like leaves falling from the trees in autumn. She told them,

> . . . In order to save them [sinners], God wishes to establish in the world devotion to my Immaculate Heart. If you do what I tell you, many souls will be saved, there will be peace. The war will end, but if men do not cease offending God, another and more terrible war will break out during the pontificate of Pius XI. When you see a night lit up by an unknown light, know that it is the sign God gives you that He is about to punish the world for its crimes by means of war, hunger, and persecution of the Church and the Holy Father. In order to prevent this, I shall come to ask for the consecration of Russia to my Immaculate Heart, and the Communion of reparation on the first Saturdays. If my wishes are fulfilled, Russia will be converted and there will be peace. If not, Russia will spread her errors throughout the world, promoting wars and persecution of the Church. The good will be martyred, the Holy Father will have much to suffer, and various nations will be annihilated. But in the end, my Immaculate Heart will triumph. The Holy Father will consecrate Russia to me and it will be converted, and a time of peace will be conceded to the world . . . [2]

Again she told them to make reparation and to pray the Rosary daily. Then Our Lady told them when they pray the Rosary to say after each mystery, "Oh my Jesus, forgive us our sins, save us from the fires of Hell, lead all souls to Heaven, especially those in most need of Thy mercy." [3]

The Lord was generous in the sufferings He sent His little friends. Lucia's mother disbelieved the reality of the apparitions; she demanded her daughter make a public apology for perpetrating a "hoax". The parish priest was puzzled. The parents of Jacinta and Francisco were inclined to believe their children's account of the visions, but were plagued by doubts as to their origin.

The people who accompanied the children to the Cova witnessed the lightning that preceded Mary's visits, and they always saw the white cloud above the holm-oak where she appeared. They believed. Word of the apparitions spread like a brush fire across Portugal.

On the 13th of August, some 18,000 gathered at the Cova, only to find that the town official had confined the seers to jail. He was determined to discourage these crowds. The jokes of his free-thinking friends, and the arrogance of newspaper editors from the cities who laughed at Fatima and its "hoax", had humiliated the little official. His cruelty to the children produced tears but no denials of their story; they were resolute.

On the 15th of August—the day the seers were released— Our Lady appeared to them and instructed her faithful children to come to the Cova the following month, and to pray the Rosary daily.

By some accounts the crowds in September numbered nearly thirty thousand. Every road and byway was filled with pilgrims searching for their Mother.

On the day of the great miracle, October 13th, 1917, some 70,000 gathered; men and women from all walks and stations in life; believers and unbelievers stood side by side. Mary directed that a chapel be built in her honor, under the title of the Lady of the Rosary. Then the Queen of Heaven displayed her awesome power. She directed her hands streaming with light towards the sun, and the sun was darkened. Then the sun began to rotate at a furious speed wrenching itself from its axis. Colors spun off the surface—red, blue, green, lighting the earth beneath. It began to zigzag, to dance; it stopped, and then plunged madly toward the crowd like a giant fireball, obliterating all else from view. People screamed for God's mercy, convinced that they were witnessing the last days.[4] Later the sun returned to its place and there was great rejoicing in this great sign, confirming the message that had been given.

But even after this miracle, the world as a whole did not believe.

There are many people alive in the world today who remember the night of the great light in the winter of 1938. The sky was reddened from horizon to horizon. Three months later, the storms of war followed the thunder of German black boots into Austria. The apocalyptic conflagration—war on a scale never imagined in the minds of men—exploded, and in its wake 50,000,000 were dead, countless millions maimed, mentally and physically crippled, homeless, hungry.

During the sixty-six years following Fatima, man in cooperation with his ancient enemy, the Serpent in the Dark, cut the Bark of Peter loose from Her moorings; She is afloat on the deep. Man did not listen to Mary's call for prayers and penance. In other times and places the Church has been attacked from without; today, the mortal enemy—Modernism—is within the gates. Basic church teachings, doctrines, and dogmas are questioned, rejected, often the object of humor. Pseudo-scholarship dissipates the Gospels. Immorality is rampant. Seminaries are bound to secularism. Catholic institutions for higher learning are often indistinguishable from their secular counterparts. Many religious orders have lost their direction. Many priests have left their flocks. Family life has disintegrated.

The Church is besieged from within and without. Modern man embraces endless "isms" manufactured in the darkened intellects of those who will not be creatures, but gods.

For the first time in the history of man, great masses of people reject the idea of God. The propulsion for this rejection is atheistic Russia. At Fatima Mary said that if man turned to his Maker, Russia would be converted, and the world would be at peace. But if man chose another path, Russia would spread her errors throughout the world, promoting wars and persecution of the Church; various nations would be annihilated, the good martyred. Where before there were none, Communist political parties exist with respectability in almost every nation. At least twenty-three nations are controlled by Communists. These nations represent one-half the earth's population. Russia neutralizes her neighbors; she foments wars in Africa, Asia, South and Central America.

Communism has one solution for its enemies—extermination. Witness the fifty million killed in China; countless millions in Russia, East Germany, Hungary, Czechoslovakia, Vietnam, Cambodia. Wherever man is bowed down with the iron of Marxism, death and destruction follow. Only Heaven can number the souls undone—killed, imprisoned, tortured by this diabolical movement.

Many voices have been raised to warn us of our plight. In 1951, Douglas Hyde, a loyal Communist party member for twenty years, and former editor of the London edition of the Communist Party newspaper *The Daily Worker*, said in an address in Lisbon, Portugal:

> . . . there seems to be no human means of avoiding a conflict which could all but exterminate the human race . . . only the knowledge that through prayer and penance the way can be found . . . Communism is diabolical. It is perhaps the most evil thing the world has ever known. . . .

Before his death in 1968, the saintly Padre Pio, a Franciscan mystic marked with the wounds of Christ, said: "I can give you only one piece of advice for today: pray and get others to pray, for the world is at the threshold of its perdition!" The great Russian Christian, soldier of sanity, lifetime student of Communism, Alexander Solzhenitsyn, said in 1976: "The situation in the world is not only dangerous or threatening, it is catastrophic!"

The same year, the man who is now Pope John Paul II, spoke to the Eucharistic Congress:

We are now standing in the face of the greatest historical confrontation humanity has gone through. I do not think the wide circle of the American society, or the wide circle of the Christian community realize this fully. We are now facing the final confrontation between the Church and the anti-church; between the Gospel and the anti-gospel. This confrontation lies within the plans of Divine Providence. It is a trial which the whole Church must take up.

On May 13th, 1981, the day and hour of the first apparition of Our Lady at Fatima, the unthinkable occurred—an attack on the life of Christ's Vicar. The following year, on the same day, His Holiness was at the shrine in Portugal publicly giving thanks to Mary for her protection and for his life and told us,

> Today, the message of Fatima is more relevant and still more urgent than in 1917 . . . it is in its basic nucleus, a call to conversion and repentance, as in the Gospel.

Like the Hebrew prophets of old, Our Lady came to Fatima to call man to prayer and penance, to battle the powers of darkness with the weapon that won the battle of Lepanto—the Rosary.

After the engines of World War II were stilled, Mary's servant Jose Thedim, the Michaelangelo of Portugal, completed his carving of Our Lady of Fatima. In May, 1947, in the presence of thousands, the Pilgrim Virgin Statue was crowned at the Fatima shrine. The image of the Queen of Heaven was borne by her faithful subjects from city to city, from church to church. Grace exploded; cures occurred; white doves miraculously appeared. Crowds were everywhere. Pope Pius XII exclaimed: "We can scarcely believe our eyes as we see the wonders she performs."

In 1947, a parish priest, Father Harold V. Colgan of Plainfield, New Jersey, was used by God to start a vast army—Mary's forces—arrayed against the forces of evil. "The Blue

Army" came into being to marshal men to prayer and to penance, to sanctify and save the human race.

Through the efforts of the Blue Army, now also called the World Apostolate of Fatima, the Pilgrim Virgin Statue arrived in the United States in 1974. In the fall of 1975, this writer became the sacred image's escort. In some mysterious way, Mary's presence is around the image. No other explanation would suffice to explain the miracles I have witnessed in my years as the Pilgrim Virgin's protector.

In the pages that follow, there is an account of the arrest of the statue by the Russians in Poland, and how the cities and towns of that beleaguered country celebrated her visit even in her absence. You will visit the lepers on Molaki Island; pray at Hiroshima; marvel at the devotion of one million Christians and Moslems of India paying homage to the Mother of God. You will travel to the Holy Land, and to the Vatican, and weep in Las Vegas when Our Lady weeps.

You will join Mary, utilizing the Pilgrim Virgin Statue, journeying through the world far and wide to bring her children back to God.

NOTES

[1]Johnston, Francis, *The Wonder of Guadalupe*, Tan Books & Publishers, Inc. Rockford, Illinois, pp. 45-48

[2]Sister Lucia, *The Message of Fatima*, Ave Maria Institute, International Press, Washington, New Jersey, pp. 30-31

[3]*Ibid.*, p. 31

[4]Miceli, Vincent, S.J., *The Antichrist*, Christopher Publishing House, West Hanover, Mass. , p. 263

I.
Beginnings

Many people have asked me through the years how I happened to be the escort for the International Pilgrim Virgin Statue of Our Lady of Fatima. Heaven specializes in mysteries; only God knows! From an early age I was blessed by God with deep faith and with devotion to God's Mother. Divine Providence provided for the nurturing and growth of that faith and devotion in countless ways. I have always been aware of the shortness of time and the length of eternity. Each minute, each hour, each day, are precious gifts from God. So I have always wanted to use my time on earth to the best possible advantage, to become what God wants me to be, and to act in harmony with His will and for His glory.

My long journey with Our Lady began with a New Year's celebration. On the last afternoon of 1972, I was having coffee with Michael and Wanda Mello in their home in Flint, Michigan. We were having a lively discussion. By the fourth cup of coffee we decided that some feast days must delight the Devil, and that New Years was one of them. We talked about the paganism in the way society celebrates the entrance of the New Year. Thinking about the drunken revelry that compounds and multiplies man's sin and misery made the coffee lose its taste. I reached for my coat.

"Why don't you come back tonight, and we'll ring in the new?" Michael said. "There's one condition—you must be here no later than 11:45."

It was the kind of night when Nature etches frost pictures on windows and pulls her diamond-studded white blanket across the land. The snow crunched and squeaked underfoot. I checked my watch under the street light—11:40. In a hurry to escape the frigid breath of the night air, I pounded on Mike's door. The neighbors' porch light snapped on. Mike, his wife Wanda, and their four teenage children greeted me.

"You're just in time to celebrate the New Year with Our Lady," said Wanda.

"And how do you propose to do that?"

"Very simple—by saying the fifteen decades of the rosary, beginning at the stroke of twelve."

These good friends seemed to be a holy contradiction to the world outside. We discussed what we should pray for. The list was endless. Finally I said, "You lead the rosary, Mike, and offer it for whatever intention inspires you."

We took our places on the hardwood floor in the darkened house, kneeling upright in front of a small statue of Our Lady of Fatima. Vigil lights made unearthly shadows. Quiet settled on us. At exactly midnight Mike began, "Dear Lady of Fatima, we are going to pray this rosary to you, and we want you to take it and use it for whatever intention you please."

At 1:20 a.m. our rosary meditation was completed. A cloak of grace wrapped our tired bodies in joy. A truly new year was beginning for me.

Some two months later I began giving talks on Our Lady. My introduction into the public forum began in my home parish of St. Mary's, Mt. Morris, Michigan. I was teaching seniors in our parish Confraternity of Christian Doctrine Program, and was trying very hard to instill in my students admiration, love, and devotion for the Mother of God. The principal of the program, Sister Thomas Mary, I. H. M., asked me to talk to an assembly of the entire high school student body. My subject, of course, was devotion to the Mother of God. As a consequence, I was invited to address the parish. Strangely enough, my talks all turned out to be one hour and twenty minutes long—the same length of time we had prayed the rosary to Our Lady of Fatima on New Years. Father Adrian, from the Pontifical Institute of Foreign Missions, heard one of the presentations and invited me to speak on Mother's Day, 1973, at his church, Holy Rosary, Detroit.

I had been anxious about speaking at St. Mary's. Feeling humanly unequal to the task, I prayed fervently to our Blessed Lady. I was reminded of the story of the priest who became a famous orator. Whenever he said Holy Mass, the church was filled with attentive listeners. A small, humble religious brother reverently served the priest. The little brother sat with his head bowed during the priest's sermons. Crowds multiplied; the fame of the priest's preaching spread far and wide. And then one sunny autumn day, when the sky was blue and the red leaves spiralled downward on soft winds, the little brother was called up to heaven. Another brother took his place. The crowds thinned, then dwindled down to nothing, for the priest's preaching was no longer powerful. Then he realized that the humble little brother's prayers were the source of his eloquence. When the Mellos volunteered to accompany me to Holy Rosary, I knew I had some good friends of Our Lady with me. I felt their prayers would obtain grace for the task.

The Church of the Holy Rosary proved to be a direct link to the Fatima apostolate. The Blue Army sent three nuns to open a school of apostolic formation at the Marian Center in Detroit. One of these nuns, Sister Mary Joseph, was interested in finding someone to speak on devotion to the Blessed Virgin. Msgr. Minck who had listened to my talk at Holy Rosary recommended me. For a year or more I drove from my home in

Mt. Morris to the Detroit Marian Center every two weeks.

To expand their apostolate, the same three nuns decided to take their school "on the road". My employment as president of a plastics corporation, a family business, made possible my accompanying the three nuns—Sisters Mary Joseph, Mary Grace, and Mary Celeste. We visited various cities and towns in Pennsylvania, West Virginia, and Missouri. While doing a school in St. Louis, I met Mrs. Lois Brown, a businesswoman who publishes a small newspaper, *The Penny Saver*, and operates St. Michael's Bookstore in the Tampa area. Because of her efforts, I was invited to speak in a number of churches around Tampa, Florida. Mrs. Brown masterfully arranged the scheduling and publicity for the ten-day tour.

A short time later the well-known Marian Priest, Father Robert J. Fox, invited me to speak at his annual Marian conference held at Redfield, South Dakota. He wrote kind words about my efforts in the *National Catholic Register.*

Friends and acquaintances thought I was getting a little carried away when I boarded a plane bound for the Netherland Antilles. I spent fourteen days constantly extolling the wonders of the Mother of God. All this was the result of attendance at the apostolic formation school in Detroit by a native of Aruba who had asked me to speak in her native land.

Upon returning home I received an inquiry from the lay director of the Blue Army, John M. Haffert, asking me if I were interested in being the escort to the International Pilgrim Virgin Statue of Our Lady of Fatima. Mr. Haffert is a man of action, and he wanted a speedy reply! I made a fervent novena to Our Lady. I prayed. I thought. I called Father Robert Fox. His advice was to leave everything and go. My most pressing concern was my mother, who was gravely ill with multiple sclerosis. If I were to go, would I be shirking responsibility to my mother? Would she understand? No one knows how deep his roots are, until he begins to pull them up. It is hard to describe the pain you feel. Should I leave home, job, family,

friends, the sights and sounds familiar to me since my child-
hood? If I did, would I be attempting to escape the responsibili-
ties of my job and family—running from the real world? Was
this pride and self-will in disguise? Was my going God's will for
me? Buried in confusion, I turned to my sister, Virginia.

"Say no, Louie. Tell them no. If Our Lady really wants you,
she'll come and get you. She won't take no for an answer."

Another escort was provided for the famous statue. The
itinerary was New York, Virginia, the West Coast area, and
then Michigan. Unexpectedly a telephone call came from a
Father Ganley.

"The escort has taken ill, Louis. Will you escort Our Lady?
Will you fill-in?" Virginia's words came back to me. "If she
wants you, she'll come and get you . . . she'll come and get
you."

After hurried preparations, I was on my way. My rational
mind kept saying, "coincidence, coincidence". According to
Father Ganley, the escort was seriously ill. Had he been
stricken in any other state, I would not have been called.
Someone would or should have telephoned the Blue Army
Headquarters for a replacement. Another "coincidence" struck
me. The Albigensian heresy in the 12th and 13th centuries
originated in a town in southern France called Albee. To
combat and dispel the evil consequences of this heresy, St.
Dominic preached the rosary. In Michigan thirteen miles from
my home, on Highway 13, is another Albee, the town wherein
the escort of the Pilgrim Virgin Statue was stricken. Our Lady
appeared five times at Fatima on the *thirteenth* day of the
month to beg people to pray the rosary.

As I made my way with the famous statue from church to
church in the Saginaw Diocese, I was full of joy. My world was
in springtime. About the tenth day something unusual happened. It was nearly time for the 8:00 p.m. Mass. St. Pan-
cratius Church (Cass City, Michigan) was crowded to overflowing. As I placed the statue of Our Lady in her place of honor, I

glanced at the congregation. A woman beckoned me. Assuming she wanted a priest or an altar boy, I glanced around.

"I want you," she whispered.

"What now?" I thought as I made my way down the aisle toward her.

"May I ask a question?" she asked, looking me full in the face.

"Of course," I smiled, wondering.

"Are your parents both living?"

What a strange question, I thought. "My father is deceased; my mother is living."

This information prompted another question. "What condition is your mother in?"

"She is an invalid with multiple sclerosis."

"And who takes care of her?"

"My three sisters and I, when I'm at home."

"Why don't you hire a nurse?"

I was beginning to wonder if the woman was a little unhinged. She seemed to read my thoughts with a sharp glance of her intelligent eyes.

"She requires around-the-clock care; the cost is prohibitive."

Without hesitation she continued. "I am a registered nurse. If you take the statue of Our Lady and spread her message, I will take care of her and charge you nothing." I could hardly believe my ears.

Later that same evening I telephoned my sister Virginia and told her the story. She was strangely silent. "Virginia, are you there?"

"Yes, yes, Louis, I'm here."

"Will you call this lady?"

"You know I will."

Some ten days later I again telephoned and Virginia answered.

"Louie, you won't believe what I'm going to tell you. That

lady is an angel. She's here ten hours a day and looks after Mom and talks to her as though Mom were Christ himself. I couldn't believe anybody could be so good; I thought she had to be an unearthly being sent by God . . . I really did. One day I couldn't resist—I put both my hands on her forearm and pressed so tightly she cried out, 'Virginia, what are you doing?' I told her, I want to see if you are real flesh and blood."

"Louie," Virginia continued, "You really have to go now. Our Lady did call you, and just like I said, she won't take no for an answer."

And so my long years of journeying began.

II.
Demons

Word finally came that I was now officially the escort of the Pilgrim Virgin Statue of Our Lady of Fatima. Like a young colt in the spring, I wanted to run, to leap and to bound. No more doubts. The die was cast. The future looked bright ahead of me. I started my new vocation in a blaze of enthusiasm.

"I'm now the official escort," I confided to a certain person. He turned and stared. His eyes caught and held mine. He moved closer. Placing his hands on my shoulders he continued staring. A menacing look rose up in his eyes.

"You will pay the price. Satan will never leave you. He will attack you physically and spiritually."

For a moment I was transfixed, caught up in his dramatic response. Is he trying to frighten me? This is all nonsense. He's wild, really wild. My mind raced. Things like this don't happen to ordinary people. The whole idea is preposterous. It's downright funny. I masked my almost uncontrollable urge to laugh aloud with a very sober expression on my face. What if he reads my thoughts?

"I have warned you." With that he left me.

A heavy set lady wearing a scarlet hat with massive multicolored plumes, like a battleship in full array, was heading ponderously in my direction. Here's the real world—ladies in funny hats, I mused. The side door provided my escape into the fresh air. I set off half running toward the church.

Then it happened. Struck with a massive force from behind, my knees buckled. I pitched forward. My palms burned from the force of the fall. I tried to get up, but I fell again. Struggling to an upright position was as exhausting as climbing the highest mountain. I couldn't get enough air. My mind was moving in slow motion. Was I dying? God, help me. A cold fear welled up in me. If I moved, would I fall again?

Trembling, I took one step, then another. The church door squeaked on its hinges. A few more steps. With fumbling fingers I removed the rosary from the Statue of Our Lady. I reached for her scapular. It eluded me. I reached again. Placing them both on my person, I prayed aloud, "Mother of God, help me, help me."

Should I get a doctor? Go to a hospital? They would certainly keep me for observation. Then who would escort Our Lady? Like a soft spring rain, the Virgin of Guadalupe's words to Juan Diego fell upon my frightened soul:

> Hear and let it penetrate into your heart, my dear little son: let nothing discourage you, nothing depress you. Let nothing alter your heart or your countenance. Also do not fear any illness or vexation, anxiety or pain. Am I not here who am your Mother? Are you not under my shadow and protection? Am I not your foundation of life? Are you not in the crossing of my arms? Is there anything else that you need?

"Dear Mother," I prayed, "keep me close to you. Help me embrace God's will. I don't want to be a fairweather son. Let me be steadfast in times of trouble and temptation. Guard me now from fear, from self-pity, from the designs of the Evil One. May I serve the Living God all the days of my life. I cast my care into your hands. I trust in your motherly protection."

In the coming days, I went from church to church escorting Our Lady's Statue, telling and retelling her message. Each hour was endless; each day forever. I could not retain food. To stand was exhausting. My brain seemed empty. It was difficult to think or remember. By a tremendous effort of will I forced my faculties to function. At each opportunity I wore the rosary and scapular from Our Lady's statue, begging her help and protection.

I was certain death followed my footsteps, paused when I paused, waiting, waiting. "Dear God," I prayed, "if you want me to die, Thy will be done, but I had planned on working a longer time for your Mother." Shadow-like I moved from place to place. At increasing intervals panic would rise up and almost overwhelm me.

The hours, the days, the long nights passed. Finally, I met the good and pious Marian priest, Father John Hogan, approaching a Church where I had placed Our Lady's Statue. Something moved me to confide in him. I poured out the story of my suffering in a flood. He listened with great kindness and concern. As I knelt before him on the sidewalk, he placed his hand containing his rosary on my head. He prayed long and fervently with his eyes closed and head bowed. Then he blessed me solemnly.

After a few days I again met this priest of God. He told me, "Louis, Satan did indeed attack you."

God has promised Mary, Virgin most powerful, final victory; she shall crush the head of Satan, prince of this world. My allegiance to the Queen of Heaven must enrage the enemy, for my first encounter with diabolical forces was not the last one. A few months later, on a night like so many others, it happened again. After completing preparations for an early morning flight that would take Our Lady's image into a midwestern diocese for a month's visitation, I knelt to say my night prayers. As I made the sign of the cross, a compelling force drew my eyes to my bedroom window. I stiffened. Cold terror gripped me. There pressing wildly against the window pane, were three hideous, half-human, half-beast faces, their red eyes gleaming with rage and fury. Then I heard, "This month, this month we'll have you." I clenched my rosary, closed my eyes and prayed.

The following morning, enroute to the Midwest, I had a lingering sense of foreboding. But when the plane hit an air pocket, the physical jarring distracted me from the memory of those faces. I turned to watch the first rays of the morning sun edge the great white cotton clouds with shimmering gold. The woman ahead of me was talking heatedly to her male companion, in a language that sounded like Spanish. Like a wild river torrent, the words poured out. On and on they went, running their course, until at last she tired. After a polite pause, I heard her companion say with a sigh, "All sunshine and no rain is what makes the desert." Now there is wisdom for you, I thought. Great food for thought.

"Fasten your seatbelts."

A few minutes later I was greeting the small crowd awaiting my arrival. I knew somehow that I had entered the storm center I had been dreading. Heaven alone knows what I endured in that diocese, and so it shall remain. I will only say that it was a time that tried my soul.

Housed in a rectory the last night of my stay, I had my first good night's rest in a month. I awoke refreshed and grateful to God, for it was the day of my deliverance. I was leaving with my assignment completed. In harmony with my mood, the day was peaceful and still, filled with the fresh air of the spirit. I snapped my suitcase closed, crossed the hall with light steps, and was halfway down the stairs.

A deafening noise shattered the peace and quiet. The priest and housekeeper came running. The window in what had been my bedroom was broken. Glass was strewn about the floor. Only a giant sledge hammer would have worked such devastation on the window frame. The way the window was broken was inexplicable. The upper window glass was intact. The lower window was cut in a perfect semi-circle, the same semi-circular pattern made by the devils' heads on my window a month earlier. Those three evil spirits were having a temper tantrum; they had failed to snatch me from the realm of grace.

Over the years, I have come to believe that harassment by Satanic forces is a powerful sign of the spiritual efficacy of the Fatima apostolate. I cannot say that my experiences with demons has lead me to the nonchalant attitude of the Curé of Ars, who became so familiar with the devil over a thirty-five year period that he nicknamed him "the Grappin", and on occasion ridiculed his antics! I did not see much humor in what happened in a certain Michigan rectory, when an over-sized mirror came crashing at me, clipping my trousers and splintering to pieces around me.

By far my most terrifying experience was in January, 1977. St. Mary's Cathedral, Virginia City, Nevada, was filled with those who had come to pay tribute to the Holy Virgin of Fatima, and to hear her message. To inspire the people to prayer and penance, the priest was describing the prevalence of Satanic worship in our own day. A candle burning brightly on the main altar went out, extinguished by some unseen force. As all eyes were upon it, it bent to a forty-five degree angle. When the priest completed his sermon, I took my place in the pulpit, to speak on Satanic masses. I had not spoken more than three sentences when the crowd, as if one person, gasped. The light of the second and last candle on the main altar went out. Slowly it bent to a right angle. A lady in the front pew cried out in open-mouthed terror, as a painful blow was dealt her from out of nowhere. Then a noise began, first loud, then louder, building into a crescendo like the snapping and cracking of a thousand tree branches. People clung to each other in fear.

New candles were lighted and Holy Mass completed. The crowd dispersed quickly.

Needless to say, I firmly believe what Holy Scripture and

the Catholic Church teach; that Satan and his demons, his fallen angels, are a reality. By telling our first parents they would be gods if they disobeyed their Creator, Satan established his religion. Its creed is Pride. By man's active participation in rebellion, Satan established his kingdom of Falsehood, where Sin, Death and Destruction reign. God's infinite justice is twin to His infinite love. But through the Incarnation, the focal point of history, the living God comes among us. Our inheritance in His kingdom can be restored.

Christ confirms the existence of Satan when he speaks to the Pharisees,

> . . . you are trying to kill me . . . the father you spring from is the devil, and willingly you carry out his wishes. He brought death to man from the beginning, and has never based himself on truth; the truth is not in him. Lying speech is his native tongue; he is a liar and the father of lies . . . Whoever is of God hears every word God speaks. The reason you do not hear is that you are not of God. (John 8:40, 44, 47)

God came in the flesh in Jesus, to lead us to our inheritance in His kingdom. Since Satan's rebellion is timeless, he did battle with the God-man. Large numbers of demons are revealed in the pages of the New Testament. Aping the Incarnation, they inhabited men. Christ expelled them, and even now, so do His apostles. The solemn rite of exorcism—the expulsion of demons—has its roots in apostolic times and continues in the Church in our own day. The Church affirms her belief in the demonic world in her Easter Vigil liturgy when she blesses the Baptismal waters,

> . . . may all unclean spirits, by Your command, O Lord, depart from hence; may the whole malice of diabolical deceit be entirely banished; may no admixture of the enemy's power prevail here. . . .

During the same vigil liturgy the faithful are called upon to renew their Baptismal vows,

> Priest: Do you renounce Satan?
> People: We do renounce him.
> Priest: And all his works?
> People: We do renounce them.

In the last century, the French poet Baudelaire wrote, "The Devil's deepest wile is to persuade us he does not exist."

Even modern Catholic scholars often suffer from this delusion, discounting the reality of Christ's encounter with Satan, His expulsion of demons, and documented evidence of demonic possession. In spite of the Gospel's clear distinction between sickness and possession, they label the possessed "psychiatric cases." These Modernist scholars and their followers seem to agree—as one author put it—that Jesus and Paul were simply wrong in their belief in demons.[1] Such people come to the study of the word of God with the pre-conceived opinion and judgement that there is no Devil, and he has no legions. With incredible pride they re-interpret Scripture, and by the magic of their modernism "uncreate" Lucifer and his followers. Through the thorny thickets of primordial sin, Lucifer gently pipes the "learned" into the fog and swampland of incredulity, while those with itching ears, stumbling and running, follow into the mire.

The hard truths of Christianity are not in vogue. "Feeling good" truths are in fashion. Modern man wants God's love and mercy but not His justice and judgement; God's humanity but not His omnipotence; Christ's crown but not His cross. But teaching half-truths is not the style of the Vicar of Christ, Pope John Paul II,

> Does man have within himself the strength to face with his own forces the snare of evil, selfishness and—let us say so clearly—the disintegrating snare of the "prince of this

world", who is always active to give man, first, a false sense of his autonomy, and then to bring him through failure to the abyss of despair?[2]

Men of the western world are running at great speed toward Utopia, the City of Incredulity, inhabited by strong men of the Communist world who have beat them to their destination, and who have said in their hearts, "There is no god; we are gods. With brute force we shall establish order, and control history." When finally confronted with that awful question, "God or man?", will the West answer, "Man"?

The Holy Mother of God warns us, as Christ warns us, that unless we repent, we shall perish (Luke 13:5).

NOTES

[1]Brown, R.E., S.S., "The Myth of the Gospels without Myth", *St. Anthony's Messenger*, May, 1971, pp. 47-48.
[2]Pope John Paul II, *L'Osservatore Romano*, p.1, ff, 11-15-78.

III.
1978 World Pilgrimage

St. Catherine Labouré was certain Our Lady wanted a statue made, representing the first part of Her apparition on November 27, 1830, in Paris, France, when the Blessed Virgin gave St. Catherine the Miraculous Medal vision. St. Catherine told her superiors, "This statue has been the torment and the martyrdom of my life. I should not like to appear before the Blessed Virgin before the design has been accomplished." After the statue was made, it was placed above the high altar where Our Lady appeared. Sister Catherine's last duty was fulfilled. She knew she was to die in 1876, and actually took her last breath on the last day of that year. Today she lies in state under the statue of the Virgin Most Powerful, the statue that had been the "torment" of her life.

John M. Haffert, director of the Blue Army in the U.S., which has custody of the International Statues, might sympathize with the "torment" of St. Catherine, because he has been the means of fulfilling the century-old prophecy of St. Catherine Labouré, "One day, Our Lady will be carried around the world in triumph."

After much planning and prayer, the machinery was set in motion for an ambitious, exciting venture never before undertaken. The 1978 World Pilgrimage would be the longest procession of all time! One hundred and eighty two ecstatic pilgrims would accompany the International Virgin Statue 37,000 miles around the world in 42 days! Those historic days would afford millions the opportunity to see the famed statue.

At Fatima Our Lady told the children to use the money left at the place where she appeared for a procession with her statue. Vying with one another for the honor of carrying her sacred image in procession had been the norm in Portugal in 1917. In 1978, four powerful jet engines on a D.C. 8 carried the statue around the world in Our Lady's own plane, entitled "Queen of the World."

A very small, portable altar was rigged up near the front of the plane so that Frs. Matthew Strumski of Warren, Rhode Island, Francis E. DeNardis of Boise, Idaho, and John Engler of Mahoney City, Pennsylvania could celebrate the Holy Sacrifice of Mass daily while we were in flight. Next to the altar was a stand to accommodate Our Lady's statue. Fresh flowers were taken from the various countries we visited and placed at the feet of Our Lady. Having Mary on board made the flight merry!

Our pilgrimage began 2:30 EST, April 6, 1978, in Miami, Florida, where the first pilgrims, from the Southern States, boarded. At 5:00 p.m., the huge D.C. 8 touched down gently on the runway at Newburgh, N.Y. picking up pilgrims from the Eastern States. With the Mid-west pilgrims, I carried Our Lady's statue on the plane in Indianapolis, Indiana. With great excitement, we were off to California to pick up the balance of our pilgrims in San Francisco. After a warm meal, large quantities of coffee, and introductions, we were anxious for a good night's sleep before leaving the continental United States in the morning.

Amid shouts of joy mingled with grateful tears, we were warmly greeted at the airport in Anchorage, Alaska at 4:30 p.m., EST. Hundreds of people jostled one another hoping for a better vantage point to view the statue carried in procession to a waiting caravan of cars. We were escorted to the Holy Family Cathedral where Archbishop Francis T. Hurely, D.D., and the pastor, Rev. Lawrence Farrell, O.P., concelebrated the Holy Sacrifice of the Mass, prayed a Rosary, exposed the Blessed Sacrament for adoration until midnight, venerated the statue and concluded with Benediction.

Our first penance came because of a mix-up. Rather than spend our first night in a warm, comfortable bed, we had the option of sleeping in the airport chairs or on the carpeted floor before our plane left for Nagoya, Japan at 6:30 a.m.—the longest leg of our pilgrimage, 12 hours flying time.

Arriving in Nagoya two hours earlier than the custom officials would be on duty, we had another sacrifice to offer Our Lady, but eventually we boarded buses for our hotel seven miles away. There was a soft rain which provided welcome relief from the heat. The cherry blossoms were at their zenith, a spectacular sight. Nagoya is the third largest city in Japan— over 2,500,000 inhabitants. Scarcely three out of 1,000 are Catholic.

In the early morning, buses were waiting to take us to the train station where we boarded one of the fastest trains in the world. Clipping along at 175 m.p.h. on our way to Hiroshima, we saw the morning dawn cool and green. The sun sparkled on a small creek nearby. There was dew on the grass and fog on the windshields of parked cars. On both sides of the train were patchwork fields with farm houses and barns. The rice fields climbed to the top of steep hills. The Japanese utilize every available inch of soil.

At Hiroshima we placed the statue at the epicenter where the atom bomb exploded on August 6, 1945 at 8:17a.m. It was April 12, 1978, 9:55 a.m., when we prayed for world peace at the site of the enormous explosion. Touring a nearby museum, pictures flashed us back in time to the hellish nightmare, a veritable chamber of horrors. Faceless children were ghastly sights, minus eyes, ears, lips, and noses. A mother was seen clutching her baby tightly, hoping against hope to stave off sudden death which was inevitable—both were charred from the intense heat and became mummified instantly. A young mother in the prime of her life was pictured lying on top of her two infants in an attempt to cover them from the enormous blast and cheat death, but to no avail. A father, agonizingly, looked up to heaven, holding his dying daughter, as though asking God, "Why?" A young mother sitting in the street, a dead child in her arms, refused to concede it to the other world. There were bodies mangled and burned beyond recognition, children crying their death cry, the image of a dog cast on cement from the immense light emitted by the scorching blast, a complete steel bridge that had been two miles away from the explosion twisted like straw, and complete city blocks leveled to rubble as far as the eye can see. A mother, horror written all over her face, dashed to nowhere with a lifeless infant dangling from her arms. Limbs were ripped from bodies; torsos scattered everywhere. Eighty thousand were fortunate to be taken in instant death; seventy thousand were not so fortunate, though they begged for the mercy of death to ease the consuming pain that wrapped their bodies from the fire. In thirty days the unbearable pain would wrench their souls from their bodies.

The description the Fatima children gave upon seeing the vision of hell would fit the description, it seems, of the conflagration that enveloped Hiroshima. ". . . and we saw as if into a sea of fire, and immersed in that fire were devils and souls with human form, as if they were transparent black or bronze embers floating upon every side just like the falling sparks in great fires, without weight or equilibrium, amidst wailing and cries of pain and despair that horrified and shook us with terror."

And yet, in the midst of all this destruction, one building stands alone in the eight block perimeter of the blast. The rosary had been prayed in that building every day! What a lesson this gives us that Mary can protect those who have committed themselves to her Peace Plan from Heaven.

We made a stop at the Peace Shrine of the Cathedral of the Assumption to pray a rosary for world peace. Saying farewell to Hiroshima and Japan, we were firmly convinced the future holds two options: peace in the world, or a world in pieces. The descendants of Adam and Eve have ushered in the Nuclear age. "Authoritative estimates put the number of existing nuclear warheads at 50,000, enough to destroy every city in the world many times over." [2] One MX missile in today's arsenal has 200 times the destructive power of the Hiroshima bomb. One of our B52 bombers "can carry more explosive power than was set off by all participants of World War II!" (*Time Magazine*, March 16, 1981)

The flight to Seoul, Korea, was only long enough for the celebration of the Mass and the distribution of Holy Communion to all on board. Thirty-five thousand South Koreans greeted us with songs, waving banners, and thunderous cheers. A huge procession, over a mile long, ended a short distance from the famed 38th parallel where an open air Mass was celebrated with the statue next to the altar. An all night vigil was held at the Freedom Bridge. Two thousand five hundred souls made the vigil, praying a rosary every hour.

Traveling the length and breadth of South Korea, visiting city after city, we received an overwhelming response. In the diocese of Wonju (the oldest in Korea), a priest presented me with a scroll stating, "My parishioners prayed one million Rosaries as a gift to Our Lady in appreciation for Her visit to our church." At a nearby grotto of Our Lady of Lourdes, 15,000 people crammed together, eighteen priests celebrated the Mass, and another sixty participated with the laity, as there was not enough room in the grotto for them.

At Taijon and Inchon, enormous crowds strove to get near Our Lady's image. At Pusan, two bishops, scores of priests, and dozens of nuns, along with thousands of laity, gave us a standing ovation as we paraded into a large circular auditorium with the statue. A fifteen decade Rosary in English and Korean followed.

The next stop, Taipei, Taiwan, proved to be a carbon copy of South Korea. We received a rousing welcome at the airport:

> A 182 member party of the Blue Army of Our Lady of Fatima, arrived in Taipei yesterday to bring blessings and best wishes to the people of Taiwan . . . the Catholic team was welcomed by bishops, priests, monks, nuns and over 800 faithful at the Taipei International Airport on arrival at 2 p.m. from Seoul. The welcoming party carried banners and cheered to the accompaniment of a girl's school band. The welcome at the airport lasted over an hour before the statue of Fatima was carried to a Catholic Church on Hsingheng South Road in a procession. The assembled Catholics held a service for world peace and a bright future for the Republic of China.[3]

At the Holy Family Cathedral in Taipei, Taiwan, Cardinal Yupin, with nine of the nation's eleven bishops, welcomed us in a service never to be forgotten. After the Holy Sacrifice of Mass, each American pilgrim was asked to walk out of church via the center aisle, one by one, to receive a standing ovation from the jam-packed Cathedral of exuberant Taiwanese. We went to a nearby hall where a dinner awaited us. It was most edifying that nine of the country's eleven bishops came to the Cathedral to acknowledge their Queen. All nine kissed the foot of the statue in honor of the person whom it represented.

A special truck, richly decorated with bright colored paper-streamers, transported Our Lady's image throughout the city, followed by thousands of people, causing traffic-jams every-where. It began to rain. A woman walking alongside of the truck happily handed me her bright red umbrella to place over Our Lady's statue " . . . so Our Lady won't get wet." The rain stopped. We continued through the busy streets. Little chil-dren were drawn to Our Lady's image. Some would peek and giggle; others ran along with the procession.

At Bangkok, Thailand, we were greeted by over 3,000 people, with a band, cheering school children, banners waving, cameras clicking constantly, and many weeping happy tears. Thailand is a nation of great poverty. As you travel in underdeveloped countries, you find modern cities bustling with commercial activity and affluence. The farther away you get from these centers of commercial life and activity, the more you recede in time, for in remote areas life goes on as it did thousands of years ago. There is no electricity, no running water, no sewer disposal. It is a stark contrast to the oppulence of the city. But rich or poor, sick or healthy, all are Her children. Mary's love, like Her statue, goes out to everyone.

In the tens-of-thousands, devotees of Our Lady, stood all along the way—unmindful of the scorching midday sun, and greeted Our Lady's statue as we went from Meenambakkam Airport in Madras, India, to St. Mary's Co-Cathedral on Armenian Street. The drive was eleven miles long. Over one hundred thousand people on both sides of the street greeted their Queen—a most impressive sight! Many shed joyful tears, and with folded hands, uttered "Hail Mary, Holy Mother". Others threw garlands and offerings into the float carrying the statue. The crowd was especially thick at St. Mary's Cathedral where we had a difficult time taking the statue into the church. The statue rocked as it was passed from hand to hand over the tremendous crowd blocking the entrance. The doors of the Cathedral had to be closed temporarily before the statue was installed high into a niche of the ancient altar. Dr. Arulappa, the Archbishop of Madras and Mylapore, celebrated the Holy Sacrifice of the Mass to a standing-room-only congregation. In his homily, the Archbishop said: " . . . devotion to Mary sprang from her love for mankind for which she suffered at the foot of the cross, on which her son, Jesus, had been crucified."[4]

From the Cathedral we took Our Lady's image to Our Lady of Lourdes Shrine at Perambur, where again we encountered difficulty in getting through the doors of the Church because of the excessive enthusiasm of the people clamoring to touch the statue. "No" was not in their vocabulary for this great occasion! All of this was repeated again at the Basilica of St. Thomas which was our last church to visit before I was to go alone with Our Lady's statue on to Bombay while the rest of the pilgrims would be taken by John Haffert to Cairo, Egypt. I met them four days later by taking a commercial airplane. The response in Madras was mind-boggling. It necessitated moving Our Lady's image from one church to another at 12:00 midnight in order to avoid the enormous and excitable throngs of people.

Poverty runs rampant in India. In the daytime you see places of ugliness and stench, where children are filthy from not being washed, where sickness festers and the people find it impossible to repel or rise above their plight, becoming re-signed to physical suffering. The smell of poverty hangs heavy in the air: sour, stale, dank, and dusty. There is a constant parade of the hungry and the homeless. I saw scaley legs bare except for the rags twined around their ankles; hands stained and streaked with imbedded grime; eyes darting with fear of living and of dying from the incessant strain of life as they know it. They move with a slow-shambling walk. Their monotonous life of want has dulled their reflexes and expectation.

Moving the statue at midnight revealed another view of the poor, for they slept on the sidewalk in great numbers. Their only possession, besides their thread-bare clothes, was an old newspaper to protect their faces from the pesty flies that would attack them in their sleep. A rusty safety pin was a pauper's treasure. Their emaciated bodies hungered for a morsel of food.

After saying good-bye to the pilgrims, I was on my way with Our Lady's statue to Bombay. How I wished they could have all experienced what took place the next few days. Our Lady's statue and myself were given a fond and reverential welcome by a mixed gathering of Catholic clergy and laity. In spite of the tight security arrangements at Santa Cruz airport, hordes of Christian devotées swarmed across the black top field as our Indian Airlines plane came to a halt.

Bishop Longinus Pereira and Fr. Aurelius Mashio, rector of Don Bosco's institution, waited among the thousands for Our Lady's image to be deplaned under the deafening roar of the brand new Airbus A-300 engines in the sweltering heat. Devout people belonging to many faiths spilled over the once restricted airport terminal area. I fastened the statue onto a pedestal on a special float. Scooters, motorbikes, cars and buses traveled all the way with the huge convoy, most of their passengers clicking away with their cameras.

As we wended our way to Don Bosco's Shrine in Matunga, hordes of the faithful lined the way for a glimpse of the Madonna. The green float was decorated with cream colored silk ribbons. Marigolds were strewn all along the eight mile route as people stood with prayerful submission and children ran behind.

To the sound of "O Lady of Fatima, Hail Immaculate Mother of grace, O pray for us, help us today, Thou hope of the human race," the 5,000 strong Catholic crowd sang hymns welcoming the statue of Fatima. The rich tones of the Church organ swelled in accompaniment. Cardinal Gracias crowned the statue just before it was placed on a high pedestal trimmed with blue and white lace.

   The statue was placed at a vantage point between the church and the school where a continuous flow, almost two miles long, moved in lanes of six in orderly fashion in spite of the burning sun.

   A special entrance was provided for the sick and the handicapped—almost 5,000 of them venerating the statue in the hope of a cure.

Cardinal Gracias declared that the Pilgrim Virgin came as a messenger of peace—peace by reconciliation with God.[5]

The people that came out to see the statue had to be policed by over 300 officers! Bombay would prove to provide one of the largest crowds we would have:

> Don Bosco's vast playgrounds were turned into a sea of humanity on Tuesday to venerate the statue of Our Lady of Fatima, which is on a world tour.

> Over a lakh [100,000] occupied every nook and corner to participate in the concelebrated mass at which Valerian Cardinal Gracias was the chief celebrant. Over four lakhs [400,000] thronged to see the statue during the day.[6]

Before Our Lady's image left Bombay, over one million came out to greet her! Their faith was dynamic; their zeal, infectious!

The flight from Bombay to Cairo was a long one. The pilot of the Indian Airlines jet humbly requested that the statue be unveiled on board as this was the pleasure of every curious passenger.

With great delight the pilgrims welcomed Our Lady and myself upon landing at the airport in Cairo. I'm not certain if they were more happy to see Our Lady, or I was more thrilled to be with them again. Fr. Francis DeNardis and I went to the great pyramid of Cheops, the Number One wonder in the world. History records Napoleon saying he could build a wall around France one foot thick and ten feet tall with the rock in the pyramid.

Permission was asked of President Sadat and Prime Minister Begin of Israel to grant us diplomatic immunity so that we could fly directly from Cairo, Egypt to Tel Aviv, Israel. This would be a first in the history of commercial aviation, as those two countries were constantly at war; consequently, you had to land at a neutral airport before entering either country. While we awaited a response to our request, we placed the statue in the Church of Our Lady of Fatima, Heliopolis, which is the spot where the Holy Family traditionally has been held to have taken refuge from Herod.

Prime Minister Begin granted the permission we sought. Within hours Sadat did likewise. The first commercial airline flight between the two countries was covered extensively by American TV networks. The day we flew from Egypt to Israel was the feast of the Passover!

The thrill of taking Our Lady's statue to the very soil she and Christ walked excited me tremendously. To take her image to Bethlehem, the Sea of Galilee, Cana, Mt. Carmel; to carry her over the very path she herself walked, daily, to Jacob's well; to place her image on the spot where the Angelic salutation was given her by Gabriel; to carry her in procession as we made the actual stations of the cross; and, yes, to place the statue at the site of the crucifixion.

Arriving in Jerusalem, the Patriarch of the city issued a pastoral letter, "The Holy Land, Our Lady's Land", and invited everyone to welcome the statue of Our Lady of Fatima at the Church of the Holy Savior. In his homily, the Patriarch welcomed the statue to "The City of Mary".

All three of the days in the Holy Land were exciting. All three mornings were cool and green. There is everywhere the smell of water rising from the earth, drawn through root and tendril, by an industrious sun. The sun stings our arms. It is going to be hot. Morning unravels, cars start, children shout, dogs bark. The sun rules the day and man naturally yields. The people know this and take their siestas at midday. Still the buses took us from one Holy Shrine to another. Our Lady's statue was always enthroned, prayers prayed, pictures taken; then a bit of socializing and off to another shrine.

Next stop: Rome, the Eternal City, May 1st. The pilgrimage of peace with Our Lady's Fatima statue brought an astonishing response by the people, baffled the Roman press (which thought it was a political ploy), and even caused a stir at the Vatican. The Pilgrim Virgin was greeted with unprecedented enthusiasm. An incredible 400,000 [7] people accompanied the statue in a shoulder tight procession for several miles along the Via Merulana between St. John Lateran's Basilica and the Basilica of St. Mary Major.

The tremendous response in Rome amazed organizers, but the local press gave practically no mention of the staggering number of people who participated. Instead, it criticized the demonstration as a fruitless Vatican campaign to swing the people against liberalized abortion in Italy.[8]

Pope Paul VI authorized his Secretary of State, Cardinal Jean Villot, to send this telegram:

> The Holy Father expresses deep happiness over the solemn Marian ceremonies. He hopes that Romans will continue to show their centuries-old and ardent devotion to Our Lady through Christian living, always consistent with the Gospel message.

An enormous crowd poured into and around the shrine of Our Lady of Divine Love where Cardinal Poletti, Vicar of Rome, celebrated a Mass. Ronald Singleton wrote in the *Universe* of May 19, 1978:

> So great was its gesture of love, as witnessed by incalculable thousands of pilgrims. . . . The three-and-a-half foot white statue seemed to take on a life of its own. . . . The old and young came to witness. Students mixed with military men. Tourists from every country in Europe came to pray. For two-and-a-half days this year, Rome's ration of terrifying violence gave way to peace. . . . The statue's last visit in June 1959 attracted hundreds of thousands. Now on this occasion, the promises and revelations made to three little Portuguese

shepherds seemed even more urgently apt. . . . The Holy
Father's words for the occasion were a simple and sweet
sermon, "A disciplined Marian cult expressing spontaneous
delicious sentiment and reflex of heart . . . an ideal model of
perfection . . . the model of a sublime mother, gentle,
saintly, a mirror of goodness . . . is the 'pray for us' which
should never be missing from our lips."[9]

John Muthig's article in the *National Catholic Register* of
May 21, 1978, stated:

> Young men wept. Old women shouted, "Viva Maria!"
> Teenagers shinnied up street lamps and traffic lights to get a
> better view. The excitement was caused by the arrival in
> Rome of the four-foot-high Pilgrim Virgin Statue of Fatima,
> being borne around the world on a chartered plane by 182
> American followers of the Blue Army. The Rome response
> flabbergasted organizers. . . . Rome—a city that boasts doz-
> ens of its own miraculous madonnas—turned out more than
> half a million people for Masses, candlelight processions and
> prayer vigils accompanying the statue's visit.

At 4:30 p.m., May 3, we landed on the runway at Vienna,
Austria, and took the statue to the ancient St. Stephen's
Cathedral. The sky was pale blue, the breeze welcome. People
from all stations in life made their appearance with a sense of
respect and loyalty, curiosity, devotion, or profound gratitude.
A sudden burst of remorse occasionally broke the silent veneration. The sun was streaming into the colored windows, while a
voice whispered to me, "I needed Her, I've been spiritually
stagnant." The long day concluded with a bone-numbing chill
in the air.

Arising early in the morning, we felt limp from the damp
and mist. Preparations were under way for a daring challenge
which could prove futile or dangerous. John Haffert, 35 volun-
teers, and myself set out to sneak Our Lady's statue into
Budapest, Hungary. Rolling along the hilly countryside we

were enjoying a morning of warmth and laughter, prayers and song. Our Lady's statue was encased in Her blue bunting bag, strapped in the third seat from the back of the bus opposite the driver's side. She stood high in the seat next to the window.

Arriving at the Hungarian border, guards in green uniforms trimmed with red requested everyone to leave the bus for inspection. Alone in her seat was the statue. Guards swarmed all over the bus, banging on the walls, climbing in luggage compartments, sliding mirrors on poles into remote corners. Incredibly, they did not appear to notice the four foot blue package, sitting prominently on the seat by the window. Standing beside me, Fr. Matthew Strumski murmured, "They don't see her!" "She is miraculous; if God doesn't want them to see Her, they won't," I replied. We boarded the bus and continued gingerly on our way.

Budapest was drab and dreary. The whistle of a far-off train added to the grimness. Stopping at St. Stephen's 14th century Cathedral, I was amused by the small birds flitting through the branches of nearby trees chasing small flies, while we waited in the hot sun to enter the building. A slight breeze rustled the leaves overhead as we entered the massive Cathedral. Marveling at the magnificent architecture both inside and out, I recalled the expression, "Architecture is 'frozen music.' "

We who treated the Hungarians to Our Lady received a "treat" in return. We were shown the right-hand of King St. Stephen, crowned the first King of Hungary on August 17, 1001, and who died August 16, 1038. The hand in the ornate reliquary was a hand 940 years old.

I walked down to a nearby lake where people were basking in the sun and splashing in the cool water. Children were scampering about in their play, gaunt old men were hobbling along, women were getting in their last minutes of shopping. I returned to the Cathedral, crossing a small brook with rippling water.

All on board, our bus took us through the heart of Budapest. We saw the scars on the buildings which had received the salvos from Russian guns fired from T-34 tanks quelling the 1956 revolution. It was a sickening sight and a reminder of the ravages of war.

At 9:30 p.m., back at the border, Hungarian and Russian guards brusquely ushered us off the bus for a thorough check before allowing us into the free-world. With Our Lady's image still in her same seat, the guards methodically went through the bus with six large flashlights. We stood prayerfully outside whispering Ave after Ave that they would not spot the statue. When the guards reached the back of the bus, they turned back. Suddenly, one of the large flashlights beamed brightly upon Our Lady's statue! Didn't they see her? As they came off the bus, Fr. Strumski whispered, "They didn't see her again!"

Because of the Vatican Radio broadcasting the message of Fatima, the story of the Blue Army, and our "Queen of the World" peace flight, the Russians picked up the information and were waiting to welcome us at the airport in Warsaw, Poland, at 11:15 a.m., May the 5th. Our plane was not treated like other planes using the airport. We were escorted by a military vehicle to a remote portion of the field that had never been used. Locked in our plane, stifled by the heat, we began to pray the Rosary as we waited for the Communists to decide our fate. The door opened and a young Russian officer escorted by six soldiers insisted the statue and its escort deplane while everyone else on board continued to agonize through the heat and suspense. Grasping Our Lady's image firmly in my arms, I walked down the gangway. As soon as I touched the ground, the soldiers removed the stairway. I knew I was to follow the armed soldiers into a huge military vehicle. Inside I saw it housed ultra modern electronic equipment. I was ordered to remove the statue from her casing. The officer asked, "Who is she?" "The Mother of God," I answered, hoping to provoke a response in the officer. There was silence. A painful awareness crept over me observing the Russian officer's facial expression. His heart must be as cold and hard as his face. His response removed any doubt that might have lingered. His "nyet (no!)" rent the air—I was back to reality. The statue in my arms, I was promptly escorted out of this vehicle into another with Our Lady's statue. Two lanky soldiers were stationed nearby waiting for a decision about our status. The sun felt abnormally hot as it beat down on the roof of the truck, making it almost unbearable inside. I longed for a breath of fresh air. Most certainly the sophisticated electronic gear was now in operation contacting the Kremlin. Thirty minutes dragged by. The soldiers told me to return to the plane with the statue.

Ascending the steps, I had to laugh. To think the atheistic Communists do not believe in God, yet they fear a 33 pound wooden statue of the Mother of Jesus!

Within minutes we were informed everyone could deplane, except the statue, which had to be locked in the cockpit of the plane. The keys were handed over to the Russian officer. For the next three days Our Lady's image would be entombed in a modern vault, guarded by Russian soldiers, as Her Son's body was entombed for three days in an ancient vault guarded by Roman soldiers.

Fr. Strumski, John Haffert, and I held a meeting and decided that something must be done to free the statue for the benefit of the Polish people. Fr. Strumski suggested going to Niepokolanow and using the Franciscans facilities to make a wire-outline of the statue. The Franciscans were overjoyed; they relished the idea. In hours, a 3/8 inch diameter metal form was fashioned into the outline of the Fatima statue and anchored to a wooden base. Written in Polish on the base was, "Our Mother Never Leaves Us!" Beneath was listed the four major cities in Poland noted for Marian devotion: Warsaw, Cracow, Niepokolanow, and Czestochowa.

Our pilgrims had been divided into two hotels in Warsaw. One hundred and two stayed in the Orbis Hotel, the tallest building in all of Poland (34 stories high). The remainder went to a smaller hotel nearby. Both hotels were operated by the Communists. In the Orbis Hotel they put only three Americans on a floor. Every room was bugged and some contained hidden cameras. Communist spies were everywhere. Fr. Strumski and I were under constant surveillance. Fr. Strumski came to my room on the 32nd floor to discuss our strategy. Upon entering, he placed his finger on his lips to warn me to remain silent. We wrote notes to each other. He had exciting news! Cardinal Stefan Wysznki would provide us with a reputable chauffeur who would drive us and the wire-outline the length and breadth of Poland. We had to rendezvous with our driver at 5:30 a.m.

Ted, our chauffeur, was unassuming, courteous, quiet, a good looking man in his early 50's. The morning air was nippy. In no time we were on the outskirts of Warsaw heading south at a good clip. We planned to take the wire-outline to as many churches as we could and inform the Polish people what the Russians had done. Cracow was the first stop. Cracow is a thriving city in southern Poland, on the Vistula River, with a population of a half a million. It is an ancient city, still displaying the magnificence that made it the capital of Poland from 1320 through 1609, and one of the most beautiful cities in Europe. We took the wire-outline to the Cathedral and placed it on the altar. Fr. Strumski gave an account to those present— at least a thousand! We were amazed at how the word had spread that we were on our way with the outline.

Speeding down the highway from Cracow to the south, our conversation centered on the fact that the Russians had given us an opportunity to make reparation for one of the five most common sins committed against Her Immaculate Heart: "disrespect for Her sacred images."

Katowice is a highly industrialized city in southwestern Poland with a population of 40,000. The large crowd in the Cathedral was astounded to hear that the Russians would not permit the statue to deplane! After a quick bite to eat, we headed for Czestochowa in south central Poland. Its population is 210,000. Czestochowa contains one of the oldest and most famous icon's in the world, the Black Madonna. Tradition says St. Luke painted this masterpiece on a table-top. It came to Poland on August 26, 1382. We were allowed to place the wire-outline directly in front of the Black Madonna. Cameras flicked constantly, recording the event for posterity. To 75,000 Poles, clustered together, we related the airport incident. Spontaneously, with tears in their eyes, voices quivering, they shouted in unison, "Praise be the Mother of God!" "Long live Poland!" Fr. Strumski and I both were proud of our Polish heritage. As Patrick Marnham has said:

> Before the election of John Paul II, a French observer of the Poles, speaking perhaps slightly enviously, had searched for a word to describe the quality of the Polish faith and had chosen not "traditionalist", or "besieged", or "uncompromising", but "cerebral". It is a union of spirit and intellect which marks the Poles. . . . Compared to the faithful of other nations they are distinguished by a fierce certainty which makes light of the doubts which trouble those raised in less tested communities. The Polish faith is strengthened by the oppression it faces from a left-wing tyranny. Such an ideology challenges the essence of Christianity; that is it challenges Christianity's other-worldliness and its claims for the immortality of the individual soul. The result is an increase in the spiritual strength of Polish Catholicism.[10]

We were informed by a number of people we could be arrested for what we were doing. Religious belief is defined as a form of mental illness in the Soviet Union. We made a hasty retreat to return to Warsaw, 105 miles away.

Hungry, exhausted, but elated, we arrived back at our hotel in Warsaw around 8:00 p.m. A great surprise awaited me. My second-cousin, her husband and a friend were waiting to meet me for the first time in our lives! We all hugged each other enthusiastically. Since they had not had any supper, nor had I, I asked them to join me in the dining room. To my dismay, the waiters refused to serve them. By the cut of their clothes and their appearance, they could easily be distinguished as native Poles. I was told native Poles could not be served in the main dining room but could be served on the second floor. Taking the elevator up, I told them to order whatever they wanted. They wanted ham as soon as they saw it on the menu. To my consternation, the waiter refused to serve them ham, because only Americans were allowed to have the ham! I then asked for four orders of ham and potatoes. I was flatly denied. Only one order was allowed me, so I gave my ham to my cousin and her husband. They both told me their daughters had not tasted pork chops in four-and-a-half years. The Russians confiscate all the meats. Once every two weeks a shipment of meat came to their village of Lubraniec. People have to stand in line from 4:00 a.m. until noon if they hope to purchase any available meat.

My relatives told me how difficult life was in their village because of the Communists. One cannot hold down a good job because if one attends Mass on Sunday, he automatically loses his job. They related the story of an elderly man who had been caught giving pictures of Mary to children and was arrested. After being released from jail, six weeks later, he was arrested the second time for the same offense. He has never been seen again! In order to travel within their own country, they are required to have passports and fill out special papers answering such personal questions as, Where are you going? How much money are you taking? How long will you be gone? How many are in your party? Who will you see? What will you discuss? Upon returning to Lubraniec, they have to fill out more papers answering the same questions, plus additional ones such as, Did you at any time discuss politics? Did you attend any meetings? What did you spend money on?

We learned of priests and nuns tortured by the most evil

Communists. Priests were asked to consecrate human excreta and urine into the body and blood of Christ. Nuns were asked to consume their God. Those who did not comply were tortured mercilessly and some died.

My cousin, husband, and friend had to return to Lubraniec, for they had only a three-day permit. Two hours later our pilgrimage was assembling at the Warsaw airport for departure to Berlin, Germany. In the balcony were Communist soldiers with weapons and cameras. One soldier stared at me with pitch-black eyes. I observed him and decided to challenge him to a staring contest. Within minutes, many in the airport watched the two of us. The soldier pitted his hatred against us in his bid to stare me down. He was holding a small weapon. I continued to accept his challenge, smiling all the while, and praying for Jesus and Mary to soften his hardened heart. After what appeared to be a stand-off, ten minutes later, I reached into my pocket, pulled my Rosary out and held it in my right hand high over my head smiling all the more! By this time, everyone in the airport was intent on our game. Bishop Sheen's words flashed before my mind, "The difference between the East and the West, is that in the East they want the cross but no Christ; in the West we want Christ, but no cross." Continuing to hold my Rosary high, smiling, inwardly I was praying for him, "Dear God, in the name of Jesus, through the merits of Jesus and for the love of Jesus, fill him with the Holy Spirit." In what looked like an apparent fit of rage, he turned away disgustedly. I continue praying for that Communist to this day.

About thirty minutes before we were to board, a Monsignor came into the airport very excited, saying that Cardinal Wyszynski wanted the wire-outline to remain in Poland! He, breathing fast, stated: "The Cardinal said the wire-outline will do more good than the famous statue because it will go into a different church every day telling the message."

Another historic flight was made by Our Lady's plane: the first flight from Warsaw, Poland to Berlin, Germany since

1946, through the Berlin Corridor. Again, diplomatic immunity was granted to us.

The celebration of Mass was held at St. Mathias Church in West Berlin, attended by all the pilgrims. After the services, four priests carried Our Lady's Statue to the Berlin Wall as we walked in a long procession praying the Rosary for world peace. There were plaques on the wall written in four languages: French, Italian, German and English. One read, "Seventy-two people died in this area trying to flee to freedom." Another read, "Sixty-three people died in this area trying to flee to freedom." Almost all of these unfortunate people had been shot to death.

It was on May 8th, 1978, the same date on which, 33 years earlier, World War II ended, that we left Germany to fly to Lourdes. Our landing at Tarbes airfield made history, as ours was the largest plane ever to land on that small field. We did so with a degree of difficulty.

The Rector of the Sanctuary of Lourdes came to the airport to meet Our Lady's statue and to lead the cortege to the Sanctuary, where a solemn entry was made at St. Joseph's Gate. The Pilgrim Virgin Statue was borne in procession to the grotto to a pedestal prepared just under the rock on which Our Lady had appeared to Bernadette on February 11, 1858, in Her first of eighteen apparitions.

We then carried the statue past the area of the baths to the top Basilica, just over the place of apparitions. The Basilica was packed. Our Lady's statue was in an honored place right next to the main altar for the concelebrated Mass. The following message was read from Abbé André Richard, President of the Blue Army of France:

> We could not all come to Lourdes, but we are united with you. Here in Paris we join with you at this same hour in a great celebration in the Sanctuary of Our Lady of Victories [world center of the Confraternity of the Immaculate Heart of Mary], with His Eminence the Cardinal Archbishop of

Paris as principal celebrant and homilist. We want you to
know that France is deeply moved by the world peace flight.

As we left the Basilica, two white doves, flying very low,
landed in the carrier which contained the statue. They nestled
at the base of the statue, close to Our Lady's feet. A light rain
began to fall. As we neared the bus, I had to quickly remove the
delicate mantle covering Our Lady's statue to prevent damage.
As I removed the statue, the insides of my forearms brushed
the feathers of the doves, who continued to remain in the
carrier acting like an honor guard for the Lady. Finally I
removed the statue and placed it in the bus. It was the second
time I had witnessed the miracle of the doves.

At Santiago, Spain, we held a lovely service in the huge old
church of St. James. Afterwards, we visited his tomb. The
Spanish sun was the hottest we encountered on the pilgrimage.
A local Carmelite convent learned of the statue being in the
vicinity and begged for a visit, no matter how brief. Our Lady
visited with them, through Her image, for two hours.

On May 13, the 61st anniversary of Her first apparition, we
were at Fatima walking in an impressive candle-light procession with the famed statue, joined by hundreds of thousands of
people from all over the world—a fitting climax to our world
peace tour.

There at Fatima, Bishop Venancio studied the International Pilgrim Virgin Statue closely. He surprised everyone
by remarking that he knew this to be the original statue. He
had detected where the paint had been worn off on the statue's
left foot, the ivory foot that José Thedim had made to replace
the badly worn wooden one—so worn from people kissing and
touching.

NOTES

[1]Sharkey, Don, *The Woman Shall Conquer*, Franciscan Mary-town Press, Kenosha, Wisc., p. 21.

[2]"To Be or Not To Be", Christopher News Notes, 12 East 48th St., New York, N.Y., #260.

[3]*China Post*, Tuesday, April 18, 1978, Vol. 25, No. 9601.

[4]*The Sunday Standard*, April 23, 1978, Madras, India, p. 4.

[5]*The Indian Express*, Wednesday, April 26, 1978, Bombay, India, p. 5.

[6]*Ibid.*

[7]Savitsky, Charles, *Our Sunday Visitor*, Huntington, Indiana, May 21,1978.

[8]*Ibid.*

[9]Johnson, Francis, *Fatima, The Great Sign*, Ave Maria Press, Washington, N.J., p. 128.

[10]Marnham, Patrick, *Lourdes, A Modern Pilgrimage*, Coward, McGrann & Geoghegan, 200 Madison Ave., New York, N.Y., pp. 152-153.

IV.
Return To Poland

"Is this the statue the Russians confiscated in Warsaw, Poland, last year?" "Yes, it is." "Are you the one who took the wire-outline around Poland in place of the International statue?" "I am." "Well, I just returned from Poland and everybody is walking around the market places, squares and shopping centers with a little wire-outline of the Fatima Statue."

This was told to me by a Catholic priest of Polish descent, in Los Angeles five months after I returned to the U.S. People had duplicated the wire-outline in such numbers that the "Absent Madonna", as the outline was called, pointed out the lack of religious freedom in Poland. Embarrassed, the government petitioned church officials for a return of the statue. Cardinal Stefan Wyszynski insisted that permission be granted to build twenty-eight churches before agreeing to bring the statue back. Permission was granted, so we returned to Poland with the International Pilgrim Virgin Statue in August 1979 for the dedication of the first new church, "Our Lady Queen of the World."

From August 12th to September 2nd, 1979, 108 Fatima pilgrims from every section of the U.S., ranging in age from 12 to 75, accompanied the statue to Europe and behind the Iron

Curtain. Rome was our first stop, flying on a commercial plane. At Castel Gandolfo, the Pope's summer home, John Paul II blessed us and the famous statue on August 15th. We carried the statue in a long procession, laying it at his feet. It was a hot, blistery day. From his balcony, displaying his papal flag, John Paul fixed his attention on Our Lady's image. As he addressed the gathering in the court yard, his eyes kept coming back to Our Lady. His smile was beaming, radiating gentleness, kindness, goodness, love, peace and hope.

With the Pope's blessing, we were eager to go behind the Iron Curtain. We had little difficulty entering Yugoslavia, bordering the beautiful Adriatic Sea. We drove through gorgeous country. Now and then we saw clusters of butterflies flitting about, as if to remind us that we too shall go into another dimension, another world—one that will never end.

Speeding along the winding roads we soon found ourselves in the large city of Zagreb, the capital of Croatia, located in North West Yugoslavia, containing 635,000 inhabitants. Our Lady's image was processed through the streets, wherever we parked our buses, to the first church we came to. Crowds appeared out of nowhere quickly. A Mass, Rosary, time for people to observe the famed image, and we were off to the next church or town. Everyone of the pilgrims took great delight in distributing Rosaries, Scapulars, holy cards, medals and the like to the local people. They in turn received them with grateful appreciation, treasuring each item—the glint in their eyes told you so.

The road began to rise as we approached the Hungarian border and our first incident. Russian and Hungarian border guards quickly made their presence known. When asked questions by the pilgrims, they were very curt. Seeing the three nuns, the guards became tense. The passports of the nuns were confiscated. Everyone could see there was trouble brewing as the officials began to act tough. Quite naturally the nuns felt uneasy. After a three hour delay, everyone was in suspense.

"Would you please show me to a telephone," I asked one of the officials. "What do you want with a telephone," he asked? "I wish to call the American Embassy and speak to the American Ambassador about the treatment we are receiving," I said, thinking it would encourage our release. "The telephones here will not connect with the American Embassy," he replied with disdain in a gruff voice. With an apparent delight he continued: "You have to phone from one of the cities; you can't get to a city until you can pass through the border." While the officials, three officers and a middle-aged woman sporting horn-rimmed glasses, were in conference, guards amused themselves brandishing sub-machine guns and carbines, attempting to unnerve us. We prayed.

Word finally came; a decision had been made; the nuns could not enter Hungary dressed in religious garb; it was against the law. One of the sisters cried as she removed her habit for the first time since she was professed. The sisters were given the necessary clothes by fellow pilgrims.

Back on the bus, anxious to continue on, we were detained again. Like cats toying with mice, the guards marched back onto the buses with a form that had to be completed. "How many cameras do you have in this bus?" A quick count was made; he wrote the number in his report. "How many movie cameras have you?" another hurried count: "Two." "How many tape recorders do you bring with you?" "Four." These had to be inspected. Returning to the front of the bus, he cautioned us: "No one is allowed to take pictures of the border. If you are even seen near the border with your camera, it will be confiscated."

We were on our way, thank God. Riding along the lovely roads we enjoyed the serenity of God's creation. What a contrast to the border incident. The first glimpse of the Iron Curtain is unexpected, shocking. There are two ten foot high barbed-wire fences paralleling one another with a 30 foot corridor in between filled with underground explosives. Every 150 yards was a 60 foot high tower with a guard periodically scanning the area with a powerful telescope. All towers contained weapons. Anyone trying to escape Czechoslovakia was a target for one of the over-anxious, trigger-happy guards, and a candidate for a sudden entrance into eternity. Outside of the curtain, huge dogs, mastiffs generally, were trained to kill on command. It was depressing; the entire country was surrounded in this fashion.

Entering Czechoslovakia I felt as though a pall of death had enveloped it. We learned of priests who had to submit their sermons to the atheistic communist officials in advance. What the Communists didn't like, they deleted. Should the priest deviate from the approved text, he could be arrested. All of the religious houses, convents and monasteries were now occupied by Russian soldiers. The religious were pressured forcefully to leave.

Prague is the capital and is located in central Bohemia on the Vltava River. Over a million people make their home there. We cautiously took Our Lady's statue into the designated churches on our way. No processions were permitted in Hungary or Czechoslovakia. Our Lady could not come out of her traveling container until we were in the confines and safety of a church—even this was risky. No publicity was tolerated. Only those few who happened to be in church would have the once-in-a-lifetime chance to see the image. We were surprised that we entered the country as easily as we did—but leaving it was another story!

As we approached the Czechoslovakian-Polish border at the Javorina Mountain Pass in Southern Poland, an ominous feeling grew on both buses. The scenery was some of the most gorgeous to be seen anywhere. Our buses had traveled 12 straight, strenuous hours on exacting roads requiring constant vigilance, to get to this border. We were trying to make the arrival time for the dedication of the new church in Warsaw, "Queen of the World," named after our plane which traveled the world in 1978 on the famous peace mission.

Hungry, cold and exhausted, we were greeted by the border guards at 9:00 p.m. They were cold, calculating and ruthless. For seven-and-a-half hours they deliberately antagonized us. We offered up their antagonism to God for their souls. Powerful searchlights centered on us all this time. Guards poked huge mirrors mounted on 12 foot long poles underneath the buses while other guards confiscated all 4 copies of our Czech visas, forcing us to later purchase new visas for a return through their country at added expense and time. Each bus driver would have to pay $85.00 for a new visa. The rest of us would pay a total of $500.00 for new visas. In Warsaw where the new visas would later be obtained, the Czech officials were most insulting and crass. You were truly at their mercy for should they refuse you a new visa, you would have no way out of the country.

During the seven-and-a-half hours we were held, the temperature dropped into the low 40's. We had no heavy clothing and felt the biting cold sting us, so we started the bus engines, hoping to keep warm from their heat. But the fumes were too much, so we tried to keep warm by putting on more of our light clothing. It wasn't enough and we continued to feel the cold through the entire ordeal.

Periodically a guard would come into the bus and ask some ridiculous question. One guard was drunk. He wanted alcohol from us. He became incensed when we replied we had none. He then solicited $20.00 in bribes from Fr. Strumski, threatening to arrest him for being a priest. Father had not worn his collar; the law forbade it. But the passport revealed his identity and the guard was going to benefit from it.

We made an all-night vigil rather than waste this opportunity. We meditated on a fifteen decade Rosary, announcing as the intention:

> Dear Lady, we offer this Rosary to you as you taught at Fatima when you said, "Everytime you make a sacrifice, say

this prayer: 'Oh Jesus, it is for the love of you, for the conversion of sinners and in reparation for the sins committed against the Immaculate Heart of Mary that I offer up this sacrifice.'" Therefore, we wish to offer you, through this Rosary, our hunger, our sleep, the cold, our anxieties and our frustrations.

Not one of the 108 pilgrims complained, including those as young as twelve. One of the men read the following aloud from the first page of his passport: "The Secretary of State of the United States of America hereby requests all whom it may concern to permit the citizens of the United States named herein to pass without delay or hindrance and in case of need to give all lawful aid and protection." A roar went through the bus. The laughter was good medicine.

Two guards returned to the bus asking for cigarettes. One of the ladies gave them a pack of Winstons. The guards had been drinking.

After praying the 15 decade Rosary, a great calm came over all, reminding us of the protection Our Lady promised to St. Dominic: "To all those who shall recite my Rosary devoutly, I promise my special protection and very great graces." We felt inspired to pray another Rosary at about ⁴ 14 a.m. Half-way through, the Communists decided to let us go, reminding us of another of Our Lady's promises to St. Dominic: "Those who propagate my Rosary will obtain through me aid in all their necessities."

The night's delay at the border caused us to forfeit our meals at the hotel where we were scheduled to stay in Zakopane, Poland, just over the border. Of course we had to forfeit much of the sleep too. Arriving at the hotel at 5:00 a.m., and being famished, we were offered a quick meal that consisted solely of bread and carrots. Food simply is not plentiful in the Communist countries.

After two hours of sleep, we were on the road again heading for Warsaw, 280 miles away. We had to really make time in order to arrive for the 6:00 p. m. dedication of the new church "Queen of the World" which would be consecrated on August 22nd, the feast day of the Queenship of Mary!

We were anxious to enjoy the fabulous scenery in Southern Poland but our bodies were more anxious for the sleep we needed. Moving at a good pace on the two-lane highway in the hot August sun, one-by-one, we drifted off into slumber.

After many obstacles, we arrived in the city of Warsaw, late but happy. the city has been completely rebuilt since being devastated by the Nazis in World War II. Warsaw is in the East Central part and is on the Vistula River, populated by 1,500,000 people. As we sped through the winding, narrow streets, children waved and shouted words of welcome. There was a feeling of happiness and joy in the air. We were finally going to arrive at our destination. Locating the new church, we were astounded to see the enormous crowd standing outside. Our reserved seats had now been occupied by others as thousands overflowed into all of the busy streets leading to the church. Hastily we prepared a procession to carry Our Lady into the new church. Since we were fifteen minutes late, it was decided to bring Our Lady in during the offertory procession bearing gifts from America of Rosaries, Brown Scapulars and holy cards along with the famed image.

Entering the church you could feel electricity in the air and the solemnity of the moment as tears flowed gently down the cheeks of Poles and pilgrims. The choir enhanced the ceremonious event: voices and music were raised on high to God as Our Lady was coming down the center aisle. Faces turned to acknowledge their Queen represented in this image. Eyes were glued to her beauty. As we reached the sanctuary and Cardinal Stefan Wyszynski, a priest invited me to place the statue on the altar prepared to the right of the sanctuary. There, I was stunned to see the framed wire-outline Fr. Matthew Strumski and myself had taken around Poland the year before. Tears of joy could not be restrained; they fell unashamedly as I placed the statue alongside of the "Absent Madonna." It was an electrifying moment. It was a historical moment.

Cardinal Wyszynski consecrated the new church with great joy. Before the day was spent, a priest from the chancery office added to the exuberance of our celebration, informing the cardinal that the long awaited government permit to build a new seminary in Warsaw had been granted.

We noticed there were now no Russian flags to be seen anywhere. Ever since the Pope's visit to Poland, the flags had been taken down and the Polish workers threatened to stop work in protest if they reappeared. How ironic that a year earlier on May 5th, the Russians stopped us and forbade the statue admittance into the country. May 5th was the very day that Pope Benedict XV began a novena to Our Lady, in 1917, to implore Her intercessory power in bringing peace to a world gone mad. Eight days later She appeared at Fatima with Her peace-plan from God: prayer, penance, reparation. How ironic that the month of May was the month Russians arrested the statue, the very month She made Her first apparition at Fatima; and that October would be Her last apparition at Fatima, and the month that She would give us a Polish Pope! One recalls to mind Pope Pius XII's words, "We can scarcely believe what we are seeing with our eyes, the wonders she performs."

We were in Czestochowa for the celebration of the 697th anniversary of the Black Madonna on August 26th. Our Lady of Fatima's image was carried through a mass of over one million people—an astonishing crowd—and placed upon the main altar containing the famous Black Madonna. What a contrast: Our Lady of Czestochowa, one of the oldest devotions of Our Lady, and Our Lady of Fatima, one of the newest. The Lady of Czestochowa, black with age; the Lady of Fatima, white with newness, reflecting that springtime of the church which will surely come after the purification of sufficient hearts.

Fr. Strumski offered the Holy Sacrifice of the Mass with over one million Poles surrounding. As you looked out over this mass of humanity, you could see the suffering they had known from the Nazis and the Communists. Suddenly they all became one gigantic face with a crown of thorns resting on the head— the suffering . . . the Mystical Body of Christ. In the "Cloud of Unknowing", a 14th century mystical treatise, we read: "God's friends always bear themselves with simple grace . . . a modest countenance, a calm, composed bearing and a merry candor." This was the picture they projected; it was contagious. Indeed, a good number of the Polish people walked on pilgrimage from Warsaw to Czestochowa, a distance of 110 miles, sleeping in fields, barns and hay-lofts.

The beautiful services at the national shrine completed, Our Lady was in my hotel room. Within minutes there was a gentle rapping on my door. A little Felician Nun, graced with a precious smile, pleaded: "Please, please, can we have Our Lady for just one hour?" Taking a quick look at my wrist-watch, I saw it was 5:00 p.m. "I really don't relish letting Her out of my sight, especially with all of the Communists in this area." "Oh, we will watch her; nothing will happen." I was won over by her simplicity and purity-of-heart and agreed to "one hour," thinking all the while that I would stay with Our Lady's statue until the one hour was up.

There were 40 Felician Nuns in the convent, all traditionally clad. They were like little children gathered around the Christmas tree when I unveiled their present. I placed Our Lady's image on a large oak table covered with a white embroidered cloth. It was masterfully done; it was the nicest cloth they had, and it must be used for Our Lady. I mentioned to the sisters how gorgeous this piece of work was. "Nothing is too good for Our Lady" came the replay. "And when She is gone, we will always have this precious cloth knowing that Her image graced it."

Once the statue was enthroned upon the table of honor, in

the sanctuary, and the hour was up, the good sisters pleaded to keep the statue for an all night vigil. "She wants to stay with us; she will not be pleased if you take her now." All forty of the kind nuns were begging as I pretended to refuse, but all the while I knew I couldn't say "no." I gave in with this stipulation: I must remove her by 6:00 a.m. the next morning, no matter what! At 5:55a.m., rubbing the sleep from my eyes, I entered the convent after a brisk walk from the hotel, five minutes away. I was surprised to see the chapel crammed with people from all walks of life. The Angelus bell pealed loudly indicating Our Lady had to be on her way. "Please, please, Mr. Kaczmarek, one last request. Can we sing a farewell song to Our Lady?" I was sorry I granted the permission fifteen minutes later when they were still singing the song, which had eighteen stanzas!

We left Poland and breezed through Czechoslovakia and Hungary and on into Yugoslavia to our port of debarkation: Milan, Italy. All along the way through the Communist countries—going and coming—Our Lady's statue was encased in her blue traveling bag sitting upright next to me in the first seat of the bus. In the front of the statue, on the floor, was the five foot red carrier that we used to carry the statue in processions. All of the Communist guards would ask "What is this thing?" "A carrier," I would reply. "What do you use it for?" "You use it to carry things." "Like what would you carry with it?" "Whatever you wish." "How many people are needed to carry the carrier?" "Four." "Can you carry luggage on it?" "If you want to, you can." Almost all of the guards would stare at the bright red carrier, scratch or shake their heads and leave. It seemed miraculous that not once did they ask what was in the four foot tall blue bag behind the carrier.

At Milan, while preparing for departure for the U.S., we made a visit to the Cathedral. The square was filled with communists holding a meeting, and they were most vociferous. I asked one of the men who understood their language what they were screaming about. "Religion." he said. "It is more beneficial to the masses for people to be working than to be wasting time in churches." Our Lady's words came to mind, "Russia will spread her errors throughout the world . . . "

There is not a single country in the entire world where the seeds of atheistic communism have not been planted and nurtured. It is the greatest evil the world has ever had thrust upon itself. Atheistic Communism has never been stronger nor more anxious to flex its muscle. Yet Christianity has never been weaker, nor more reluctant to live the Gospel message.

When our 747 Jumbo-Jet touched down at Kennedy Field in New York, everyone on board burst forth spontaneously with "God Bless America." I saw people kiss the ground. One of the pilgrims, Mrs. Elaine Atiyeh, said "let anything happen to the United States of America, but God forbid it should ever fall to Communism."

V.
Images

Under the sponsorship of the Blue Army, the Pilgrim Virgin Statue, the image of the Mother of God as she appeared in Fatima, Portugal, has been crisscrossing continents, stirring the hearts and minds of people everywhere to hear and heed the gospel message—the call to prayer and penance.

For many reasons, some people use the word "idolatry" to refer to the Catholic use of sacred images. These people recoil from statues of Mary, and angels and the saints, and even from the figure of Christ crucified. Because the Pilgrim Virgin Statue in our time is an instrument of God's grace to men through Mary, it should be helpful to review briefly the history of sacred images in worship.

One of the scriptural passages most frequently quoted to oppose sacred images is this:

> I, the Lord, am your God, who brought you out of the land of Egypt, that place of slavery. You shall not have other gods besides me. You shall not carve idols for yourselves in the shape of anything in the sky above or on the earth below or in the waters beneath the earth. (Exodus 20: 2-5)

But in the same book, the Lord tells Moses:

> Make two cherubim of beaten gold for the two ends of the propitiatory, fastening them so that one cherub springs direct from each end. (Exodus 25:18-19)

Since God is not contradictory, it is clear that He forbids strange gods and idol worship of any kind. No person, thing, or idea shall supplant God's primacy. At the same time, God specifically directed that images of angelic beings were to be made to adorn the propitiatory, which was placed on top of the Ark of the Covenant, the very place where God promised to meet with Moses. From earliest times, then, God was pleased to encounter man in the presence of sacred images.

It is hard to believe that there are still people who believe that Catholics worship statues. Do Americans worship Robert E. Lee, or George Washington? There are statues of historical personages throughout the civilized world. Such works of sculpture create in citizens a sense of historical continuity, reverence, and love of homeland. In this way they contribute to the stability and order of the state. Statues of religious subjects also create for the people of God a sense of historical continuity with the Church's pilgrimage in time. They inspire religious reverence and devotion, and move people to virtuous acts.

What Christian is not moved with sorrow when viewing the Pietà—the sorrowing Mother with her crucified Son? We are filled with the hope of salvation when gazing at Michelangelo's massive figure of St. Peter. We feel the protecting arm of God in the figure of St. Michael the Archangel. The figures represented in sacred images are the figures of beings who inhabit Heaven, the final destiny of faithful Christians, their eternal homeland.

On the other hand, to find Idolatry we need not look to sacred images. Power, Money, and Lust are contemporary idols whose temples of worship are filled to overflowing.

A rejection of religious images grows out of man's rejection

of his own creaturehood. God created man's body from the dust
of the earth, made him a part of the natural world, the world of
matter. He endowed that material body with five senses. God
himself became a part of that matter in the Incarnation, the
central point of history. G. K. Chesterton states it well:

> There really was a new reason for regarding the senses and
> the sensation of the body and the experiences of the common
> man with a new reverence . . . It had hung upon a gibbet. It
> had risen from the tomb. It was no longer possible for the
> soul to despise the senses, which had been the organs of
> something that was more than man . . . Plato might despise
> the flesh; but God had not despised it. The senses had truly
> become sanctified.[1]

From its earliest beginning until the present time in history, the influence of the ancient anti-life religions of Asia has
plagued Christianity, particularly in the form that attempted to
blend the pagan and Christian beliefs. Manicheism held that
nature, the world of creation, the world of matter of which man
is a part, is evil, associated with darkness, and created by Satan.
Good is associated with the spirit and light. Begun by the
Persian prophet Manes in the century after the death of
Christ,[2] the wild fire of Manicheism, billowing smoke and
fumes, licked the gates of Christendom and sent sparks cascad-
ing over her walls, sparks that ignite heresy. In the eighth
century, the Iconoclasts rose up, led by Leo the Isaurian,
Emperor of Constantinople. The Iconoclasts believed that
sacred pictures and images made worship impure. Pure worship should not lower itself to associate with things of the
senses. As a result, the churches were stripped, their art
demolished.

The Manichean influence continued and fathered many
errors in Western Christendom. In the 12th and 13th centuries, the moral and social structures of northern Italy and southern France creaked and groaned to near collapse under the gale

winds of Albigensianism—a Manichean heresy. The Albigensians believed man's purpose in life was to free himself from the world of matter, i.e., darkness, evil. While the Church teaches that purity leads to fruitfulness, on the natural or supernatural levels, the Albigensians began depopulation by means of the great lie—purity is sterility. Marriage was forbidden, and suicide permitted, in fact, encouraged. Here is Leo XIII's description:

> Carrying the terror of their arms everywhere, they extended their sway far and wide by massacre and ruin. . . . [But] God in His mercy raised up against this scourge, a man of great sanctity, . . . [the] Father and Founder of the Dominican Order. . . . [T]his hero, quickened by the Spirit from on high, did battle with the enemies of the Catholic Church . . . not with violence and force of arms but with the utmost faith in that devotion to the holy rosary which he was the first to introduce and which his followers carried to the four corners of the world. [3]

Through St. Dominic, Our Lady of the Rosary dampened the fires of heresy with a rain of grace, and led her people back into the bright sun of God's creation, to praise Life, to praise Being, and to praise their Creator. The Manichean spirit surfaced again during the 16th century.

Luther, the Augustinian monk, weighed down with revulsion at the corruption of morals, the greed and indolence of the clergy, the externalism of religious practice, reacted by teaching that man was radically corrupted. Man's will is useless, his reason useless, and his good works meaningless. According to Luther, man was incapable of resisting evil; he rejected the idea of holiness and sainthood. In one fell swoop he abolished the saints, monasticism and the Mass.

During the Reformation, Iconoclasm was raised from its eighth century grave. Here is Fr. John A. O'Brien's account:

The destruction of images was revived by Luther and the
other Reformers of the sixteenth century. The churches and
monasteries were the great museums of the art of the Middle
Ages. Many priceless paintings and statues were demolished, frescoed walls were whitewashed; and gorgeous
stained glass windows with figures of Christ and His saints
were ruthlessly smashed. The iconoclastic campaign was
especially vehement in Germany, Holland and the British
Isles. A traveler to these countries, visiting some of the
desecrated Catholic churches which are now being used as
Protestant houses of worship can scarcely fail to note the
mutilated statues of Christ and the saints still standing in
their niches.[4]

Under the new Manicheanism, religion became a drab and
colorless business. The joy and richness of man's art—his
noblest attempts to recreate and mirror the beauty of the
Eternal—were scorned.

Although the Reformers were motivated by zeal to purify
the worship of the Church they unfortunately chose to use the
destruction of art, music, and holy images as a major part of
their methodology.

It is essential to understand that when God created man,
He did not make a pure spirit, but a creature of spirit *and*
matter: "The Lord God formed man out of the clay of the
ground and blew into his nostrils the breath of life, and so man
became a living being" (Genesis 2:7). The material senses of
man's body fuel the faculties of his soul—his intellect, his will,
his memory. The early church understood the value of images
using them to teach the truths of the faith. Today, the need for
symbols and images continues; we need to return to our
churches, our statues, our pictures, our traditional stations of
the cross. The most effective media today—television—makes
vital use of these truths. The mentors of Madison Avenue know
that a picture is worth a thousand words.

Yet some still are suspicious of the use of sacred images.
Clinging to negative emotions about the Church gives rise to

false notions about her teaching and practices. Throughout her history, the Catholic Church has consistently and adamantly forbidden the worship of images. Catholics pray to Mary, to the angels and to the saints. They worship God alone.

Just as the destruction of religious images was in times past a violent exterior manifestation of Christian disunity, the acceptance by Christians of images and symbols in religious worship will be a sign of genuine inner unity.

Mary, the Mother of God, appeared in Fatima, Portugal, in 1917 to warn man that he is poised on the razor edge of the bottomless abyss. The image of Mary, Our Lady of Fatima, has been viewed by hundreds of thousands of people. Will this image of the Holy Virgin be the sign under which all Christians everywhere re-unite?

A part of the Catholic world, as well as Christians in general, have kept Mary under a cloud for centuries. John Henry Cardinal Newman observed:

> Catholics who have honored the Mother still worship the Son; while those who have now ceased to confess the Son, began by scoffing at the Mother. [5]

During the same period in history, Father Faber writes,

> Here in England Mary is not half enough preached. Devotion to her is low and thin and poor. It is frightened out of its wit by the sneers of heresy. It is always invoking human respect and carnal prudence, wishing to make Mary so little of a Mary that Protestants may feel at ease about her. Its ignorance of theology makes it unsubstantial and unworthy. It is not the prominent characteristic of our religion which it ought to be. It has no faith in itself. Hence it is that Jesus is not loved. . . . [6]

Dr. Lacy, a Methodist minister, sounds the keynote for ecumenism of the future:

It is devotion to the Blessed Mother that helps unite us as Christians. When Protestants lose their wide-spread hangup that Roman Catholics have worshipped and do worship her, they can perceive by the power of the Holy Spirit an authentic ecumenism that calls us "to be one". When many Roman Catholics stop apologizing for their emphasis on her in order not to offend the Protestant community, they can put her back where she rightfully belongs. . . .[7]

In the beginning God tells Satan, "I will put enmity between you and the woman, and between your offspring and hers; He will strike at your head, while you strike at his heel" (Genesis 3:15). Maximilian Kolbe, a sainted prisoner of Auschwitz, emphasizes the role of the woman of Genesis for our own day:

Modern times are dominated by Satan and will be more so in the future. The conflict with hell cannot be engaged by men, even the most clever. The Immaculata alone has from God the promise of a victory over Satan.[8]

NOTES

[1]Chesterton, G. K., *St. Thomas Aquinas, The Dumb Ox*, Image Books, Doubleday & Co., Garden City, N. Y., 1956, p. 118.

[2]Danielou, J. & Marrou, H. I., *The Christian Centuries*, McGraw-HillBook Co., N. Y., 1964, Vol. 1, p. 192.

[3]Leo XIII, *Supremi apostolatus* (Sept.1, 1883), quoted in the Benedictine Monks of Solesmes, *The Holy Rosary, Papal Teachings*, translated by Oligny, Rev. P. J. OFM, St. Paul Editions, Boston, Mass., pp. 46 and 47.

[4]O'Brien, Rev. John A., *The Faith of Millions*.

[5]Newman, quoted in the preface to St. Louis De Montfort, *True Devotion to Mary*, Montfort Publications, Bay Shore, N.Y., 11706, p. 11.

[6]Fr. Faber, Preface, p. 12 (see note 5).

[7]Lacy, Dr. Donald Charles, *Devotion to Mary Should Transcend Denominations*, The Criterion, July 22, 1983.

[8]Franciscan Marytown Press, Kenosha, Wisc., *Immaculata Magazine*.

VI.
Miracles

The beloved disciple, St. John, tells in John 2:1: "There was a wedding at Cana in Galilee, and the mother of Jesus was there." Because of Mary's sympathetic concern for the needs of the bride and groom at the wedding, she told her Son, "They have no more wine!" (John 2:3) As a result, Jesus worked the first miracle of his public ministry.

Ever since, Mary's generous and Immaculate Heart has been interceding for us in heaven. Nine centuries ago, St. Bernard went so far as to advertise her intercession in his Memorare: "Remember, most gracious Virgin Mary, that *never was it known* that anyone who fled to thy protection, implored thy help, or sought thy intercession was left unaided!"

Down through the centuries, at the famous shrines and through her images, Mary has been chosen by God to be the means by which many miracles and cures have been performed.

In my travels with the Pilgrim Virgin Statue, I have personally known and witnessed many occasions in which Mary has shown her motherly kindness and affection to those who come into the presence of the Pilgrim Virgin Statue to pray to her, to pay her homage, and to beg her intercession.

In relating the following cases, of course I am not anticipating the official judgment of the church on any of these cures or graces. I do not use the term "miracle" in a technical sense; but I am witnessing, like the apostles, to things that I have seen and heard.

Many times God uses cures of the body to reach our souls. Here are some examples of physical cures that have taken place:

Springfield, Massachusetts, 1977. A distraught mother carrying a little boy approached the Pilgrim Virgin.

"My son cannot walk," she told me. "The doctors say he has a tumor on the brain. It affects his equilibrium; he is so sick." She touched the boy's hand to the foot of the statue.

Ten days later in another church the same woman came to me with tears of joy and said, "Praise God! My boy is cured! The doctors say the tumor is gone!"

On October 27, 1978, a Father John Ruba, O.P., who was then teaching at Providence College, telephoned me. A woman he knew had followed my footsteps in the Providence area. Each day, wherever the Pilgrim Virgin journeyed, she followed praying unceasingly for her son—a man in his early twenties. The doctors had told the woman that her son would die shortly unless he under went surgery for the removal of a brain tumor and that the tumor had grown in such a fashion that when they removed it he would become a vegetable. Father Ruba continued that the doctors cut into the upper portion of the young man's skull in order to remove the tumor. The skilled hands of the surgeons were not needed, for the hand of God had touched the young man. The tumor had vanished.

In Fargo, North Dakota, a woman suffering from epilepsy for twenty-six years was cured in the presence of Our Lady's statue on June 1, 1981. In the same diocese a man told his pastor, "I was sitting in the church praying to the Mother of God, my attention riveted to the Pilgrim Virgin Statue. I felt a strange sensation. An icy cold gripped the upper portion of my

lungs and slowly spread through them. My sixteen year struggle to breathe is over. My emphysema is cured."

On a balmy March 23, 1979, in Tustin, California, a man in
his early thirties, Thomas Beevers, was cured of blindness in
the presence of the same statue. Not only did God give sight to
his eyes but—more importantly—to his soul, for he sobbed, "I
will never sin again. Tell people wherever you go to the wonder
of this day."

The parish bulletin, St. Mark's Pittsfield, Massachusetts,
dated April 19, 1981, Easter Sunday, carried the following
item: "St. Mark's parish will host the statue of Our Lady of
Fatima from the shrine in Portugal. Because of the devotion to
Our Lady which the presence of this statue encourages, many
answers to prayers and miraculous healing have occurred. This
was the statue that was here in 1977 at the ceremony at the
Common when the Pastor was healed of a cancerous tumor."

In the vestibule of St. Jude the Apostle Church, St. Petersburgh, Florida, a lanky 16 year old boy approached me quickly:
"You're with the statue. I saw you in another church." He
trembled, speaking with a grave voice: "They killed my buddy.
He was 17. He wanted out." "Out of what?" "The cult. We
worship Satan. I want out too. They kill babies—they sacrifice
them to Satan."

He was so earnest as he spoke that his face was pale and
strained and his breath came in gulps. I weakly said, "Stay away
from them." "If I don't show, it's no go." "I don't understand
what you are saying." "They'll kill me too . . . that is the kind of
cult I am in."

"Put on the Brown Scapular of Our Lady of Mt. Carmel and
place yourself completely in her hands."

Three years later the same lad saw me in Inverness, Florida, at Our Lady of Fatima Church during a patter of light rain.
"I went to the next meeting and that Brown Scapular that you
touched to the statue of Fatima and placed over my shoulders
fanned the little spark of courage so that I boldly told the

Satanists I belong to Jesus and Mary. I walked out. They all stood there motionless and helpless—paralyzed—as I walked between all of them without their laying a hand on me. It was because of the Brown Scapular which I deliberately wore on the outside of my clothing for all to see."

Entering the lovely country church of the Immaculate Conception in Madison, Ohio, on a sultry day in June, Mrs. Albert Dingle was diligently preparing the gorgeous flowers, roses and carnations, to place around the altar awaiting Our Lady's statue. "Did you hear what happened when you were last here with the Lady's statue in April of 1980?" "No." "After the noon Mass, you were dismantling Our Lady's statue when a young mother, who had recently become a widow, came up with her three children to pray in front of the statue. She apologized for being late and started to take her children and leave. You said, 'No, that's all right, I'll leave Her here, you just go ahead and pray.' While they knelt there, two friends of mine, Betty Elmore and Phyllis Petroff, happened to be standing on either side of the statue. I was nearby but saw nothing."

"As the two women stepped down from the altar, and started to walk toward the back of the church, one turned to the other and said, 'Did you see what I think I saw?' The other said 'I was just going to ask you that same question. I think I saw Our Lady smile at those children praying there with their mother.'"

"About two years later, Betty was cured of abdominal cancer, and Phyllis became a Vincentian Nun at 52 years of age."

"Betty's doctor had told her she would have to go through years of chemotherapy after her operation, and was astounded when giving her a checkup to find the cancer gone! He said, 'Betty, I know you had cancer, I had it in my hand.'"

On a picture perfect day, leaving St. Augustine's Church in Barberton, Ohio—where they have had Perpetual Adoration of the Blessed Sacrament since Ash Wednesday, 1960—a Mr. & Mrs. Donald Coffman and their four small children extended their hands in gratitude and friendship along with an envelope containing a note which read, "On September 9th, 1984, at the National Shrine of Our Lady of Lebanon, The International Pilgrim Virgin not only touched our lives but changed them . . . we are now going to daily Mass, and through Mary's intercession, are trying to aid in saving sinners."

In St. Edward's Church, Ashland, Ohio, six red roses arranged beautifully with baby breath carried a card reading "To Honor the Blessed Mother." It was signed by Mrs. Helen Kudley, who actually witnessed the miracle of the sun at Fatima on October 13, 1917—she was a young lady, 17 years of age, at the time. Later, Mrs. Kudley spoke, her voice breaking several times and her eyes swelling with tears as she described in detail the great miracle of the sun; the conversion of many sinners; even the animals present which fell to the ground as though in reverential awe. Before the day ended, a man left church whispering, "Thank you Lord for the graces of this day."

Under a beautiful, star-speckled sky, Delbert Bingham stopped to chat with me in Minnewaukan, N.D. "I had a miracle! I suffered for 20 years with damaged lungs caused from trying to rescue my five sons who perished in a fire when our home burned down." Sitting in front of the statue, Delbert said he felt as if ice were slowly going through his lungs, the sensation lasting about a minute. "And immediately I was cured!" Extending the conversation further, I found out that Delbert had also lost a child in infancy. Cheerful and serene, he left me with these words: "God has six of my children—I have the other six!" I was astounded at this humble, beautiful and exemplary submission to God's Will.

A Mrs. Gail Carlson of Beltrami, Minnesota, shared with me her lovely experience. "The last time you were here with Our Lady's statue, I was praying, asking Our Lady for the conversion of my Methodist husband, Dwain. I heard a voice tell me to pray for my own conversion first!" Dwain joined the church in December of that year.

Andrew J. Mitzel of Casselton, N.D., had exploratory surgery in March of 1981. High grade cancer of the bladder, the fastest moving type, was discovered. A second operation in June of that year was to remove the bladder and give him a urostomy. During the operation the doctors discovered it was too late. They closed him up with a prognosis of three months to live. He had to start cobalt treatments, which numbered forty-seven in all. Following these, more exploratory surgery was ordered. On the way in to the operation room, Andy said "the doctors are going to be surprised this time." The doctors were amazed! The large tumor in the bladder was gone. Several tissue samples were taken showing an all clear sign. Andy attributed all of this to the visit of Our Lady's statue after he had touched its foot. Andy, in June of 1982, was given another cross: bone cancer. He never complained. He offered all of his sufferings to Our Lord and His Blessed Mother for the sins of the world. He would not allow anyone to remove his Brown Scapular; and he said the rosary several times a day. There was a glow about his body and a smile on his face as Our Lady came for him on Saturday, August 14, 1982.

In West Chazy, New York, a young man approached me as I stood beside Mary's image.

"My brother is in a coma and has been for over ten months."

"What brought it on?"

"He fell from a moving truck. The doctors can't do any more. They tell us just to wait. They don't give us much hope."

I touched a brown scapular to Our Lady's statue. "Give this scapular to your brother."

Later the young man said, "As soon as I put the brown scapular on him, he opened his eyes, and called my name, his first word in almost a year."

The mother who watched her Son's blood stain the wood of the Cross as the sharp nails pierced His flesh, feels human suffering, knows anguish of spirit. In our sorrow and wretchedness she reaches out to us; and through her powerful intercession foreshadowed at the wedding feast of Cana, she intercedes with our Savior. With the water of His redemptive grace she renews the life of our body and soul. The miracles of grace that pour forth upon us from our prayers to the Mother of God in our veneration of her image would fill volumes. Here are some firsthand accounts.

A parish priest in a mid-western city told me of a soul he encountered during the Pilgrim Virgin's visit in his church. A woman in her mid-fifties saw the Pilgrim Virgin Statue on the television screen. Although she hadn't been to a Church for years, she found herself going to see the statue. As she saw the image, something inside her opened. She found the confessional and poured out her sins to God.

Two hours later the woman was dead. Through the intercession of the Holy Mother of God, she returned to her Father's house—the last year, the last month, the last day of her life.

Although it is some seven years ago, I remember as though it were yesterday what happened in a church in the Boston diocese during the Pilgrim Virgin's visitation there. The pews were filled; people stood in the aisles. To my dismay, I discovered after my first sentence that the microphone was not functioning. I thanked God for my strong lungs and prayed to Mary that the congregation would hear her message. I closed, as usual, by saying that anyone who wished could come up and venerate the statue. I was certain I had been heard, for the first person down the center aisle came from the farthest point—the vestibule. His torn sweatshirt and grassy jeans hung on his lanky frame. No wonder all eyes were on him with his beard stubble, his long, matted, greasy hair and one toe protruding from his sneakers. Foul is the only word that described his odor. Within a few feet of me he stopped and shouted, "What's this all about?"

The ushers were at his side ready to throw him out. I motioned them back.

"What's this all about?" he shouted still louder.

"This is the image of the Mother of God," I whispered. "This is the Pilgrim Virgin Statue of Fatima; her name is Mary. This is the way she looked when she appeared to three children in Portugal. She came from Heaven to tell us we must stop offending God by sin, and that we must pray and she will help us to be good and bring the world back to God."

"Can she help me?" he whispered.

"Yes," I replied.

"What do I have to do?"

"Pray, and ask Our Lady for help."

"I don't know how."

"Kneel with me before the image and repeat what I say." Without hesitation and with a look of wonder he knelt beside me. We began,

"Hail Mary full of grace . . . "

"Hail Mary full of grace . . . "

When we finished our prayer he stood peering into the face of the statue. After a few minutes, he turned quietly and left the church. The time was 8:45 p.m.

Later that evening the pastor told me, "We had a miracle of grace here tonight. Around 9:00 p.m., there was a knock at the door. I found a young man who looked like a vagrant standing at the entrance. He blurted out,

"I want to become a Catholic right now!"

I invited him in and he explained his demand.

"I'm a junkie, a doper. I didn't have any religion. Except I guess maybe you could call atheism some kind of religion. I was on my way to pick up a load of dope down the street from here. When I was passing your church, I heard this voice. It drew me just like a magnet. It pulled me in. I stood in the back and from there I could see the statue of a woman, and the preacher, when he got through, said we could go up and look at her. Something drew me right up there. I couldn't resist. I demanded an explanation. I was a little shook, I guess. The man explained things and got me to pray with him. Then I really looked at the statue. Right then and there I wanted to change my life. I can't tell you anymore, but here I am."

In the area of Boise, Idaho, a parish priest told me he heard the confession of a man who had been away from the Church for forty-two years. The priest asked his penitent why he returned to the practice of his religion and this is his explanation.

"I was at the airport earlier today. A bishop, some priests and about a hundred lay people were apparently waiting for someone. I was curious. Then one of the passengers from an incoming flight approached them. There was excitement in the air. This man carefully unzipped his carry-on case. The crowd looked on expectantly. They began singing and waving banners, happy as children. He carefully unveiled the most beautiful statue of Our Lady. He placed a jeweled cloak around her and a crown upon her head. They sang louder. I moved closer. It was a great moment of grace for as I saw her face, I wanted to come back to be close to God and His mother again. I joined in their Hail Marys."

One evening after visitation services, I witnessed God's grace dissolving hate, hate buried thirty-five years deep, feeding upon itself. In its place grace poured the oil of sorrow and forgiveness and the light of joy. Tears wet the old man's cheeks as he told me his story. "I came here from my motherland Poland." My heart warmed to him, for I too have deep roots in the land of my ancestors. "I came here with nothing, nothing but hate. It gave me the will and energy to survive. All my family died in Auschwitz. Unspeakable deeds were done there. Deeds that filled my sleep with nightmares and my days with bitterness. But today for the first time in thirty-five years, the Holy Virgin by the grace of God gave me light. I must banish hate from my heart or be an exile now and forever. This day I am free from the poison of hatred. Thanks be to the good God." He wiped his tears and smiled at me.

One of the Church's greatest needs in our time is for devout religious: religious faithful to the Gospel, faithful to prayer and penance, faithful to the Vicar of Christ. St. Louis De Montfort tells us that where the Holy Spirit finds Mary in a soul, He enters that soul completely. Vocations will blossom in parishes where there is great devotion to the Mother of God. Many, many parents have told me that their sons and daughters have embraced religious vocations following the visit to their parish of Our Lady of Fatima. These young souls drawn by the Mother of God to the service of His Church understand the French poet Paul Claudel's statement: "Youth is not made for pleasure but for heroism."

In some instances the working of the Holy Spirit is especially poignant. I recall such an incident in a New York diocese. Some young people told me they were praying earnestly for a friend. They grieved over her frequent bouts with dope, her flagrant indulgence in sexual immorality, her refusal to listen to their warnings. No amount of pleading would change her. Finally they challenged her to view the Pilgrim Virgin Statue which was then in their parish. I witnessed the young woman viewing the sacred image. As she stood in front of the statue, such grace was infused into her soul that her face was transformed visibly and mysteriously. Two years later I returned to the same parish. The young woman was not in the congregation; she was in a convent—the cloistered Carmelites.

The disintegration of the family is of grave concern to Holy Mother Church. A partial litany of spiritual disorders includes a 700 percent increase in the divorce rate in this century; one divorce for every 1.8 marriages; skyrocketing illegitimate birth rates; a tripling of the suicide rate in ten to fourteen-year-olds in the past twenty years; steadily climbing violent crime rates. Thirteen million children live in households with one parent or no parent.[1] Dr. Armand Nicholi, affiliated with Harvard Medical School, points out

. . . Christian Churches have been responsible for much of
this disorder by their passivity, silence, and ambiguous
teaching.[2]

The evidence is all around us, for those who have eyes to
see and ears to hear. Christian eyes and ears should be able
to recognize and identify the workings of the world, the
flesh, and the devil in the midst of our fallen, blinded society. It is a society which, in the words of Pope John Paul II,
has set out on "the programme of man's death".[3]

We reap the whirlwind of secularism, of modernism.
Where shall we turn? John Paul II answers, " . . . Mary will
remain the one to whom God entrusts the whole of His mystery
of salvation." Families who turn to Mary, hear the clear call
from Fatima; they daily invoke her in the prayers of the rosary.
Through her they find her Divine Son and boundless grace to
live out their solemn commitments.

Many times in my journeys I have met families who come to
view the Pilgrim Virgin Statue out of curiosity; the publicity
surrounding the event attracted them. Mary rewarded their
curiosity with the bounty of the Queen of Heaven—the grace
to return to the practice of their faith.

There is no doubt that Our Lady of Fatima is gathering
souls for her Son when she visits a parish. After a visitation one
priest in a diocese of the Upper Peninsula of Michigan wrote:

> I am giving more instructions than I've ever given in my
> thirteen years as a priest, more confessions, more returns to
> the Church. I see more going to Mass and Communion
> regularly, more Christian charity. [4]

A coordinator from a diocese in New York writes,

> All churches were filled to capacity, many, many to over-
> flowing. Our Lady blessed us with the longest procession . . .
> one mile long and an hour in length—through the busy
> streets of our largest city. . . . The traffic was stopped on busy
> Hempstead Turnpike at 7 p.m., and as the procession passed

the people on the streets blessed themselves, knelt down or just stared in sheer delight . . . [5]

A priest in a diocese in Massachusetts told me,

I have learned more from this visitation than I have from anything in all my priestly life. [6]

Fr. Anthony Noviello of Holy Rosary Church, Wilkes-Barre, Pa., said in the February-March, 1984, issue of "Life and Family News,"

I was so pleased to read your account of the International Fatima Statue. I brought Our Lady to 27 churches in one month. The priests and people said it was the greatest spiritual event in the history of our diocese! It was tumultuous; simply unbelievable what Our Lady did to the diocese, and what we initiated: the devotion to Our Lady of Fatima; novenas, tridua, part-night and all-night vigils which are still being continued. . . .

Fr. Donald J. Grainger of Holy Spirit Church, Huntsville, Alabama, in the February, 1984, issue of "The Little Messenger" stated,

The three days in our parish have been like a spiritual retreat—so many blessings have come to us, and as the statue continues through our deanery and the diocese, I am sure many blessings will come upon our people.

In June of 1984, after having had the famed statue three times in ten years, Fr. Edward McCullough of St. Procopius Church, New Salem, Pa., said,

There have been countless blessings and graces in our diocese in preparation for, during and following the visitation of the International Pilgrim Virgin Statue of Our Lady of Fatima.

Mother Angelica had Our Lady's famed image and myself on her Eternal Word Television Network on January 25, 1984. In the "Monastery-Network Times" Spring issue of 1984, she stated, "So many phone calls came in that the program was extended another half hour."

And in her Newsletter of April, 1984, she stated, "Even my own sisters received a boost in their love for Mary during the program with the Pilgrim Virgin of Fatima."

To write the wonders Our Lady has performed in her visitations would fill volumes. I know with St. Louis De Montfort that I have experienced "her motherly kindness and affection."

Mary is reaching out to all souls who truly seek her Divine Son. While Our Lady's statue was in the Pensacola, Florida area, I had the opportunity of broadcasting by radio a thirty-minute presentation. I invited people of other religious denominations to view the statue of Our Lady. The program was replayed the following week by popular demand. Some two weeks later a priest from Pensacola told me that 52 people of other denominations requested instruction in the Catholic faith.

"Meanwhile God worked extraordinary miracles at the hands of Paul. When the handkerchiefs or cloths which had touched his skin were applied to the sick, their diseases were cured and evil spirits departed from them" (Acts 19:11-12).

"My boy is cured, my boy is cured," were the happy words that bounced off of the walls of St. Finbar's Church in Burbank, California. The excited Mother had touched her twenty-year-old son, stricken with bone cancer, with a rosary that had been touched to the statue.

"I felt a heat on my lip and I knew the cancer was gone," were the startling words of a young lady in Willow City, North Dakota who touched a rosary, which had touched the statue, to her cancerous lip.

When Moses was leading the Israelites out of Egypt and

they complained to him for doing so, and for the wretched food and the lack of water, the Lord punished them, sending saraph serpents which bit the people so that many died.

> Then the people came to Moses and said: "We have sinned in complaining against the Lord and you. Pray the Lord to take the serpents from us." So Moses prayed for the people, and the Lord said to Moses, "Make a saraph and mount it on a pole, and if anyone who has been bitten looks at it, he will recover." Moses accordingly made a bronze serpent and mounted it on a pole, and whenever anyone who had been bitten by a serpent looked at the bronze serpent, he recovered. (Numbers: 21:7-9)

Seeing the statue in Sacred Heart Church, Tampa, Florida, prevented a despondent woman from committing suicide. Intoxicated with grateful appreciation she told me she now saw her life in its proper perspective putting God first, others second, self last rather than the reverse, as she had done previously.

Msgr. William C. McGrath, P.A., in his book *Fatima or World Suicide* states:

> Accompanying the International Pilgrim Virgin Statue [as the first escort], two things I have learned during the course of a Fatima Pilgrimage that has already taken me into more than forty dioceses in these United States. First of all, the countless unceasing miracles of grace, whereby sinners have returned to the sacraments in almost everyone of the nine hundred parishes visited, are evidence of the fact that the Blessed Mother is calling her own children back to the wounded heart of her Divine Son, in preparation for whatever may lie ahead in the uncertain days before us. In their thousands, to the amazement of priests from end to end of America, they have returned to the sacraments after having been out of the Church from 5 to 50 years. Repeatedly I have been told that nothing like this has ever happened before and it is idle to seek for any merely human explanation. The second thing I have learned is that the little people are

keenly aware of the significance of the Age of Mary. They
have been bitterly, almost cynically disillusioned by our
human leadership and now, in their millions, they are turn-
ing not to Big Fours or United Nations but to Mary, the
Mother of God. (p. 19)

A Mrs. Judy Vargas of Providence, R.I., told me that when
Our Lady's statue visited in November of 1980, her son David,
11 years of age, had been in a coma for five and one half days at
Rhode Island Hospital. She asked for a Brown Scapular
touched to the statue. Within one hour, after having placed it
upon her son, he came out of the coma.

At St. Martin's Church in Amarillo, Texas, in January of
1985, a three and a half year old boy asked his mother, as the
statue was being carried out of the church in procession:
"Mommy, where did all the Angels go?" all the while looking
up at the ceiling.

A Vietnam veteran was fighting his greatest fight in St.
Joseph's Church, Bay City, Michigan. After much anguish he
approached me: "I was an atheist until I looked into her face—I
don't see how anyone could look into that face and not believe
in God." He was at Mass in the morning kneeling beside me.

Sometimes, too, God shows his sense of humor. In the back
of a convalescent home in St. Petersburgh, Florida is a small
lake that is enjoyed by about fifty white ducks. While I was
speaking to the residents and nurses my train of thought was
distracted by a commotion in the lobby. The little, white-
feathered creatures were being chased out of the building by
personnel wielding brooms. They had made an attempt to visit
Our Lady but were promptly ushered out. We had our first
miracle of the ducks!

Father Michael P. Bafaro, pastor of Our Lady of Loreto
Church of Worcester, Massachusetts, told me that while he
was in Rome, Italy, in 1950 he had assisted a woman, apparently undergoing mental problems, to the statue. She was screaming and flailing her arms. Upon touching the statue she fell limp

and peaceful, back to her normal self again.

One of the most stunning cures I witnessed occurred in Holy Rosary Church, Wilkes-Barre, Pennsylvania. During the talk a middle-aged man limped into the packed church and squeezed himself into the front pew directly in front of the statue. His anguished face betrayed the excruciating pain his body was suffering from the cancer that was slowly eating away his life. Groans and moans removed any doubt, disturbing everyone.

Immediately after Mass, he hurried into the sacristy anxious to share the tremendous news—the pain was gone! He was to have a new lease on life. "My sister told me to come and see the Lady, that she would help me." With mixed emotions— joy, tears, shock—he continued "Our Lady knew how I suffered. She is so good and I am so bad. I am a terrible sinner."

Several years later I returned to the church and inquired about the man. The pastor said "He is a model Catholic."

In St. Mary's Church, St. Louis, Missouri, a man of average height and robust build, asked me "Do you remember me? I placed my hand on Our Lady's foot when you had the statue in Gary, Indiana last year. I begged for a cure of my leukemia." "Yes, yes," I replied rapidly, anxious to hear what he had to relate. "I have gotten worse. I know this is the last time I'll see the Lady until I see her in Heaven. I came to thank her for the grace of resignation to God's will." With that he knelt in grateful prayer.

NOTES

[1]Martin, Ralph, *A Crisis of Truth*, Servant Books, Ann Arbor, Michigan, Chapter 10, p. 164.

[2]*Ibid.*, p. 165.

[3]*Ibid.*, p. 167.

[4]Brodeur, Rev. E., St. Stanislaus Kostka Parish, Marquette, Michigan, U.P.

[5]Atiyeh, Mrs. Elaine, Internatonal Pilgrim Virgin Visitation Coordinator, Rockville Center Diocese, New York.
[6]Pastor, Parish Church, Springfield Diocese, Massachusetts.

VII.
Sacramentals

The Cardinal's stately presence filled the standing-room-only church as he approached the statue and reverently kissed the Rosary and the Brown Scapular, a reminder that these sacramentals too are part of the Fatima message for peace in the world, and that they have not been discarded by Holy Mother Church since Vatican II:

> This most Holy Synod deliberately teaches this Catholic doctrine and at the same time admonishes all the sons of the Church that the cult, especially the liturgical cult, of the Blessed Virgin, be generously fostered, and the practices and exercises of piety, recommended by the magisterium of the Church toward her in the course of centuries be made of great moment, and those decrees which have been given in the early days regarding the cult of images of Christ, the Blessed Virgin and the saints, be religiously observed. [1]

Cardinal Luigi Ciappi, who served as theological adviser to five popes, was in Cleveland to celebrate Mass at St. Rose Catholic Church as part of a visit to six U.S. cities. This eminent theologian was gracious enough to celebrate Mass during the appearance of the statue of Our Lady of Fatima, and was not ashamed to show his veneration for both the sacred image and the sacramentals associated with it. We can be sure that his response was based upon the most impeccable theological grounds, as well as the gift of piety.

Pope Paul VI elaborated further on the teaching of the Vatican council cited above when he appointed Cardinal Silvas as his legate to the Santo Domingo Marian Congress in March, 1965:

> Let the faithful hold in high esteem the practices and devotions to the Blessed Virgin approved by the teaching authority of the Church in the course of the centuries; . . . the Rosary of Mary and the Scapular of Carmel are among these recommended practices. . . . The Scapular is a practice of piety which by its very simplicity is suited to everyone, and has spread widely among the faithful of Christ to their spiritual profit.

In singling out the Rosary and the Scapular for particular mention, Pope Paul brought to our attention the two major sacramentals of the Fatima message. Of the two, the Rosary comes first to mind, for did the Lady not say, "I am the Lady of the Rosary" (October 13, 1917)—truly a significant statement in view of the numerous titles Our Lady has at her command! Historically, the Christian people have turned to the Rosary when the world was threatened.

All of Europe was saved through the Rosary when the proud Ali Pasha and his Turkish hordes threatened to wipe out Christianity. Pope St. Pius V pleaded for the recitation of the Rosary to help the outnumbered Christian fleet. Christian soldiers literally boarded their ships with a Rosary in one hand and a lance or sword in the other.

Don John of Austria led the Christians to a victory at Lepanto on October 7, 1571, in one of the greatest naval battles of all time. Because of this great Rosary victory, October 7 has been named the feast day of the Rosary.

Six hundred thousand Rosary-praying women rallied on March 19, 1964, in Sao Paulo, in response to the Archbishop of Rio de Janiero's pleas to heed Our Lady of Fatima's request for prayer and penance, and the atheistic Communists fled Brazil on April Fools Day—"The fool has said in his heart there is no God."

Soviet Russia gobbled up as many countries as she could after the cessation of World War II. One country that she entered, and occupied a great portion of, was Catholic Austria with a population of 7,000,000. In 1948, under the zealous work of Father Petrus, the Austrians agreed to put Our Lady of Fatima's peace plan into operation. Ten percent of the people prayed the Rosary daily and offered the sacrifices demanded by their daily duty as penance.

Seven years later, on May 13, 1955, the Communists announced they were leaving Austria, a country strategically located, with great mineral deposits and oil reserves. The Austrians, in 1955, accomplished through the peace plan of Our Lady, without shedding one drop of blood, what the Hungarian Revolution failed to do with guns, just one year later, at the cost of a blood-bath of 135,000 lives.

Theresa Neumann, the stigmatist of Konnersreuth, Germany, said the Russians, who had broken 53 pacts with other countries, pulled out of Austria because the people prayed the Rosary. Truly the Rosary is the most powerful weapon for peace in the history of the world. Father Patrick Peyton said, "The Rosary is the most powerful weapon we can take into our hands." When Bishop Sheen was asked to describe the power of the Rosary, he replied, "There are just no words to describe the power of the Rosary!" Padre Pio referred to the rosary as his mighty weapon.

"My Mother's Rosary saved my life!" said the poised and outgoing Rev. Canon Bronislaw Szymanski of St. Adalbert's Church, Providence, R.I., as he continued talking about the tremendous power of the Rosary. On Sunday, April 7, 1940, the German Gestapo began massive arrests of all intellectuals in the Suwalki and neighboring villages of Poland. He was one of 30 priests arrested. His new residence: Dachau Concentration Camp! "There I existed as a number, #22544," for five years—under the most unbelievable conditions of life—he was not sick one day. He was not only spared from malaria after being exposed to it, but from the poisonous injection of infected blood into the veins of his legs for experimental purposes. During his five years in Dachau, 1,300 Polish Priests met a martyr's death.

In 1959 he was reunited with his mother. With a heart overflowing with joy and gratitude, she told him he was liberated from the hands of Hitler's executioners because of her Rosary:

> My son, when I found out that you were in the concentration camp, I prayed the Rosary every day and spoke to the Blessed Mother thus: "Heavenly Mother, you knew the suffering & tortures of your own Son, being scourged, dragged and carrying the cross on which He gave up His earthly life. I am a Mother, and my son suffers hunger, beating, torture and hard physical labor in a concentration camp. I beseech you Blessed Mother that I may see my son healthy once more."

In 1831 Frederick Ozanam arrived in Paris to begin his university studies at the Sorbonne. He was eighteen years of age. In the midst of rowdy students, with scenes of corruption before his eyes, he felt that his faith was trembling like a little flame about to go out. One evening he went into a church and caught sight of a man kneeling in a corner and praying a rosary so devoutly that his crisis of faith vanished, never to return again. The man who was praying the rosary was the great professor, scientist and inventor, Professor Andre Marie Ampere, whose name has become immortalized in the electrical industry through terms of "amps" and "amperes." The eighteen year old Ozanam went on to become the founder of the St. Vincent de Paul Society.

Frederick Ozanam lived until the age of 40. He died in the odor of sanctity. He loved to tell anyone who would listen, "The example of Ampere acted upon me more than all books and sermons put together."

Joyce Kilmer, famed for his poem "Trees," often used to skip his lunch hour and dash over to Holy Innocents Church on 32nd Ave., New York City, and, with ink-stained hands, kneel before the Blessed Sacrament praying his Rosary.

St. Teresa of Avila tells us how priceless a treasure is just one Hail Mary. Shortly after her death, she appeared to one of the sisters of her community and told her that she was willing to return to a life of suffering until the end of time just to merit the additional degree of glory with which God rewards one devoutly prayed Hail Mary.[2]

A Father John Baptist Packianather of Tuticorin, India, told me that "The Rosarians have prayed a Rosary 24 hours around the clock, daily, in front of the Blessed Sacrament since February 2, 1928 in Shri-Lanka" (formerly Ceylon).

The Popes have been lavish in their praise of the Rosary, and in the encouragement they have given to the faithful to recite it. From the year 1402 until the present, every single Pope has spoken out on the power of the Holy Rosary or written an encyclical upon it. There have been 513 papal pronouncements on the Rosary! No other devotion in the history of Catholicism has been so highly sanctioned by Papal authority.

Every modern pope has stressed the importance of the Rosary in his teaching. "Pope Pius XII stated that the Rosary is the remedy given by Heaven 'for the healing of the evils which afflict our times.'" Pope Paul VI devoted almost one-third of his encyclical *Marialis Cultus* to the relevance and importance of the Rosary. And Pope John Paul I, while Cardinal Patriarch of Venice, taught the following:

Namaan the Syrian disdained the simple bathing in the Jordan. Some do as Namaan saying: "I am a great theologian and a mature Christian, steeped in the Bible and in the liturgy through and through, and they talk to me about the rosary." Yet the fifteen mysteries of the rosary are also the Bible and so are the Our Father, the Hail Mary, and the Glory Be—they are the Bible united to prayer that nourishes the soul. A Bible studied on the mere level of investigation could only nourish pride and empty it of its value. It is not rare for specialists of the Bible to lose their faith.[3]

Pope John Paul II lost no time in saying "The rosary is my favorite prayer," at his Angelus message on October 29, 1978. He has been encouraging the rosary ever since.[4]

The second sacramental emphasized by Our Lady in her Fatima message, the Brown Scapular, was mentioned in a thirteenth century prophecy by St. Dominic to Brother Angelus: "One day, Brother Angelus, to your Order of Carmel the Most Blessed Virgin will give a devotion to be known as the Brown Scapular, and to my Order of Preachers She will give a devotion to be known as the Rosary. And one day, through the Rosary and the Scapular, She will save the world."[5]

At Fatima She would appear, for the first time in twenty centuries of apparitions, holding a Rosary and a Brown Scapular. During the great "Miracle of the sun" on October 13, 1917, she appeared in the final vision, dressed as Our Lady of Mount Carmel, implying that her children should be similarly clad.

The Scapular has the approval not only of the Vatican Council Fathers, but also of the Bishops of the United States, who in their Pastoral Letter "Behold Your Mother," name two of the popular "practices," the Rosary and Scapular:

> We view with great sympathy the distress our people feel over the loss of devotion to Our Lady and we share their concern that the young be taught a deep and true love for the Mother of God. We Bishops of the United States wish to affirm with all our strength the lucid statements of the

Second Vatican Council on the permanent importance of authentic devotion to the Blessed Virgin, not only in the liturgy, where the Church accords her a most special place under Jesus her Son, but also in the beloved devotions that have been repeatedly approved and encouraged by the Church and that are still filled with meaning for Catholics. As Pope Paul has reminded us, the rosary and the scapular are among these tested forms of devotion that bring us closer to Christ through the example and protection of His Holy Mother.[6]

On the anniversary of the Seventh Centenary of the Brown Scapular, in a letter to the Carmelites, Pope Pius XII said, "The modern form of devotion to Mary is Consecration . . . the Brown Scapular is a sign of that Consecration to Mary."[7]

The uniform of a policeman, soldier, sailor, nurse, judge, or religious is undeniably something more important than the garment itself. A police officer's badge is but metal with a design upon it, but no one would question the power and authority that go with that badge. The American flag is a cloth symbol we proudly display as citizens of our country. In a similar way, the Brown Scapular is a sacred cloth symbol that we are a child of Mary:

> The Scapular is a sign of our special adoption by the Mother of God. The first and the greatest privilege it brings is that it envelops us in a special love of Our Blessed Mother. It makes us "Hers" in a very special way. She repeats to us the words of the prophet Ezekiel: "And I passed by thee and saw thee: and behold thy time was the time of lovery: and I spread my garment over thee and covered thy ignominy. And I swore to thee, and I entered into a covenant with thee . . . and thou becamest mine" (Ex. 16:8).[8]

Historians say the single most discussed event in American history is the Battle of the Little Big Horn,[9] but few know that it contains an amazing scapular incident. On May 17, 1876, the

7th Cavalry Regiment, led by General George Armstrong Custer, left Fort Abraham Lincoln in Mandan, North Dakota, for a date with destiny, 400 miles to the west: the grassy hills and gullies of the Little Big Horn in Montana.

Less than five weeks later, Custer and more than 200 of his soldiers would be dead, scattered in groups on a grassy ridge overlooking the fast flowing Little Big Horn River, their corpses bloated after a battle in smoke, dust, and confusion.

Among the lifeless, bloody forms, one body was especially respected and shown preferential treatment by the Indians. It was that of Colonel Myles Keogh, a Irishman of deep Catholic faith. His body was propped up against one of the few trees in that sparse area. Colonel Keogh's tunic had been torn open; there carefully and neatly disposed by savage hands, was the Scapular of Our Lady of Mount Carmel.

> The American correspondent of *L'Univers* commented that "without doubt the Sacred Badge awakened recollections of the teachings of some devoted missionary; one could see that several of the savages had assisted in bearing the body of an enemy, only a few moments before an object of detestation, to a sheltered spot; there placing it in a reclining position, the head leaning against a tree, they had carefully arranged the Badge, so loved by the deceased, upon his breast."[10]

Though all of the soldiers had been massacred, and hundreds of horses perished in the melee, one horse came out of the battle alive: Commanche, Colonel Keogh's charger!

Wherever Our Lady goes through her image, she offers bliss not sorrow. Hers is a voice that kindles hope, not bleak despair; a voice that tells mankind to look up, not down. Her words give hope to an increasingly hopeless world. She assures us that if we do penance, honor and consecrate ourselves to Her Immaculate Heart, and receive Holy Communion in reparation to her Heart on the five first Saturdays, she will bring peace to our world. Hers is a peace plan that cannot fail, for its author is God.

An integral part of this peace plan is the use of the spiritual "weapons" she holds out to us: the Rosary and the Scapular. Worldly wisdom disdains them. But the history of mankind's political, military and intellectual efforts has shown that peace is not possible without listening to God and following His will. In the final analysis, peace is a gift from God. Man cannot achieve it on his own. Clothed in the "uniform" of the Scapular, and armed with the "weapon" of the Rosary, we will be able to overcome all spiritual forces that come against the peace of the world, and our own peace.

When Lucia was asked if the Scapular is as necessary in fulfillment of the requests of Our Lady of Fatima as the Rosary she replied: "The Scapular and the Rosary are inseparable."[11]

NOTES

[1]*Dogmatic Constitution of the Church*, St. Paul Editons, Boston, Mass., 02130, Chapter 8, paragraph 67, p. 68.

[2]*Fatima, Rosary, Scapular*, Marian Guild, Box 565, Joliet, Ill., 60434, p. 2.

[3]Johnson, Francis, *Fatima, The Great Sign*, AMI Press, Washington, N.J., c. 1980, p. 107.

[4]*Ibid.*, p. 107.

[5]Haffert, John M., *Sign of Her Heart*, Ave Maria Institute, Washington, N.J., 07882, c. 1971, p. 218.

[6]"Behold Your Mother, Woman of Faith," United States Catholic Conference, 312 Mass. Ave., NW, Washington, D.C., 20005, Chapter 4, paragraph 93, p. 35.

[7]Most Rev. Lynch, E.K.O. Carm., *Mary's Gift to Carmel*, The Friars, Aylesford, Kent, England, p. 42.

[8]*Ibid.*, pp. 11 and 12.

[9]"Custer Rediscovered," *The Bismarck Tribune*, Bismarck, North Dakota, 58502, p. 3.

[10]Carm. Rev., IV, *Chroniques du Carmel*, July 1892, p. 70.

[11]Haffert, *Op. Cit* , p. 197.

VIII.
Wonders

Of all the wonders associated with Our Lady's image, the most famous is the phenomenon of "tears."

> One could sense something was happening as everything in the Cathedral was quiet. There was no movement of any kind except a man pointing to the statue [and] a priest moving to closely view the face. I myself looked very closely and very carefully to convince myself that what I saw was true: moisture coming from the eyes of the statue. Moisture had gathered in the lower part of the eye. The only further proof I could have sought was by physically touching the moisture on the eye and cheek. This I did not do out of reverent respect for the person represented by the Statue.

This was the explanation given by Mayor William Briare as told in the *Soul* magazine, May/June, 1979, issue. The man "pointing to the statue" was myself. Eagerly I was informing the "priest moving to closely view the face" of the tears. With mixed emotions and awe, I attempted to grasp the magnitude of what was happening. Respectfully and gently I wiped her tears with a new handkerchief.

The Las Vegas Sun newspaper of Saturday, February 11, 1978, carried the stunning story of the weepings which had

taken place on January 8th, 9th, and 10th. The paper said 6,000
people had witnessed the tearing. Prudently, Bishop Norman
McFarland waited until our visitation was completed before
releasing any comment to the media. The role of the statue in
traversing the world is to bring the Fatima message of prayer
and penance, not the sensational.

On January 11th, the statue ceased tearing. On the 12th,
the coordinator of the Las Vegas Diocese, Mr. James Bellamy,
asked to take the statue to the James Marsh AMC automobile
dealership in Las Vegas as a token of grateful appreciation for
his supplying a car to transport the famed image around the
diocese during the month. After a quick introduction, I wasted
no time in asking Mr. Marsh if he would like a private viewing
of this sacred image.

In his spacious, well-equipped office, Mr. Marsh studied,
with great admiration, the details of the statue. Upon my
relating the incident of the tears, he begged permission for his
employees to see the image. Within minutes his office contained over thirty people, predominantly Protestant: clerks,
janitors, painters, salesmen, mechanics, and a notary public. It
was evident Mr. Marsh was eager to communicate what he had
just learned; it was also evident his audience would be difficult
to convince, for you could sense the unbelief conveyed by a few
feeble snickers. The setting changed dramatically when Mr.
Marsh exclaimed: "My God, she is crying now!" A stunned
silence fell. A voice asked, "Why is she crying?" Another voice
cried out a public confession, "Because of me! Because of the
sinful life I am leading!"

In the presence of the employee who had just publicly
confessed, I asked that Mr. Marsh and all of his employees sign
a statement saying they had witnessed this phenomenon,
notarize it and submit it to our Headquarters. They were kind
enough to do so. As I prepared to remove the image, tears
continued to flow from the eyes of the repentant person.

After asking many people, including priests, nuns, and

professional people, what they thought the reason for the shedding of the tears was, the majority cited the legalization of prostitution in a number of Nevada Counties. Warning against impurity is certainly part of the Fatima message. Our Lady warned us, "Certain fashions will be introduced which will offend Our Lord very much." Pure little Jacinta also said, "More souls go to Hell because of the sins of the flesh, than for any other reason."

The Las Vegas incident was my first direct experience of the Statue shedding tears. My second experience took place in Carthage, New York, at the home of Mr. and Mrs. Alfred D'Angelo.

May 7, 1980 was one of those lovely spring days that you think to yourself, "It's great to be alive!" as you fill your lungs with a breath of fresh air. Birds were chirping to God's glory, flowers were springing up everywhere in many colors, sizes and shapes to do Him honor, and the sun was shining brightly to teach us we should let the Son shine in and through us, if we are to be other Christs! However, inside of the home Father Eugene Del Conte, Father John Robillard, the Legion of Mary members, the D'Angelos' and myself, felt the gloom of the suffering Christ, upon seeing the statue weep.

In later discussions, a number of priests spoke of devil worship in the diocese—some said it was rampant! Water flowed from the side of Christ as he hung on the cross . . . perhaps it flows again because He is still suffering for sin.

Scores of people have confronted me with, "I don't believe the statue sheds tears." Ultimately all one can tell them is what Franz Werfel, who wrote the *Song of Bernadette*, said: "For those who believe, no explanation is necessary: for those who do not believe, no explanation is possible."

In the February 10, 1985, bulletin of All Saints Parish, Manassas, Virginia, the following was published: "On Sunday, February 10th from 5:00 p.m. to 8:00 p.m. we are privileged to have in our church the miraculous International Pilgrim Virgin

Statue of Our Lady of Fatima. This statue was carved from cedar wood at the direction of Sister Lucy, the only one alive of the three children who saw the Virgin Mary at Fatima. Numerous times people have seen tears flow from the eyes of this statue. Your Pastor is one of those who witnessed this phenomenon."

There are basically two wonders which have been associated with the image itself. The first, as related above, is the tears. There have been others who have witnessed this phenomenon, but with the exception of the pastor's statement above, I have described only those incidents for which I have been a first hand witness.

The other wonder is sometimes called "The Miracle of the Doves." From the very beginning of the Pilgrim Virgin's travels, doves, the symbol of peace and of the Holy Spirit have attended Our Lady of Fatima statue wherever it has gone on pilgrimage. They fly to the statue as if drawn by an invisible magnet. Often they refuse food and drink and remain at the base of the statue for hours, even days, without leaving. It is something no one can explain.

One famous incident involving the doves also involves Padre Pio, the saintly Italian priest who bore the stigmata (wounds of Christ) on his body, and who died September 23, 1968. When the Pilgrim Virgin Statue was brought to Italy it was carried in a white and blue helicopter to the 92 provincial capitals of the nation. It was in Pisa that doves began to accompany the statue.

On April 25, 1959, Padre Pio was rushed to the hospital with an illness that threatened his life. He was so ill, that Pope John XXIII sent him a letter of condolence. Almost four months later—August 5, 1959, the statue was taken into the chapel at San Giovanni Rotundo; Padre Pio begged to see her. Two brothers aided him. Just as he got within several feet of the famed image, three white doves flew into the chapel to the base of the statue, and performed this maneuver a total of three times before finally resting at the base of the statue. Padre Pio kissed the statue and was helped back to his room. Later, from his window, he could see and hear the helicopter carrying Our Lady's Statue on its way to other visitations. Padre Pio exclaimed: "Dearest Mother, when you came to Italy I became like this. Do you go now and leave me this way?"

The pilot of the helicopter has testified that on an unexplainable impulse he turned back towards San Giovanni, where a great crowd was gathered around the Monastery, as though in a final salute. At that moment, Padre Pio got up from his bed and came to the window, where the helicopter was hovering, and through the window he waved at the Pilgrim Virgin. From that moment he was restored to health.

While I was staying at the Little Flower Haven in Pensacola, Florida, I obtained this first-hand account written for me by Sr. Mary Francis of the Little Flower:

> My experience concerning the famous statue of Our Lady of Fatima took place in the year 1949—when my assignment as a Carmelite Sister took me to Puerto Cabezas, Nicaragua, Central America. Fr. Salazar brought the statue to St. Peter's Church there.
>
> A large crowd met the plane and was astonished to see fourteen doves surrounding the statue in circular motion as it was taken from the plane. A procession formed on the way to the church and ten more doves joined those that came with the statue.
>
> The statue remained in and around our area for three days and nights. It was most noticeable that three doves remained constantly at the feet of Our Lady except for the time that they were fed. Furthermore, we witnessed the astonishing fact that two doves flew to the altar, one on each corner thereof, during the Consecration of the Mass and returned to their place on the pedestal . . . at the end of Consecration.
>
> During the daily procession through the Port, neither band music nor fireworks would frighten the doves away.
>
> Most impressive was the perfect tranquility pervading the town while the statue was there. Inexplicable was the feeling of peace that transcends our earthly mode of life. Even those

who professed no religion seemed to be touched by it. Men who had not been to Church for years returned to the sacraments. My feeling after the statue's departure was as of one awakening from an ethereal dream.

In Victorville, California, I had the good fortune of meeting a Robert Z. Saldivar. He was in the church, viewing Our Lady's Statue and listening to me speak about the miracle of the doves. He could hardly wait to speak to me. He had accompanied Our Lady's Statue on an American B-17 Heavy Bomber, flying it from Fatima to the United States Air Base at Terceira in the Azores some 400 miles west of Portugal. The doves would not be left at Fatima, but twelve of them actually flew to the Azores, and landed many hours after the plane, in order to be with their Lady! Mr. Saldivar related this story to me in July of 1978.

In March of 1985, while in the Providence Diocese of Rhode Island, Father Louis de M. Diego, Pastor of St. Elizabeth's Church in Bristol, told me that as a newly ordained priest in 1948, the year the statue visited his island of Terceira, he was one of the four priests who carried her in procession. He reaffirmed Mr. Saldivar's story of the doves, adding that they were perched in the carrier which was used to transport the statue in procession, and that 30,000 people participated.

Fr. Diego told this story exuberantly while we were eating our last meal of the day with his associate, Fr. Antonio de Sousa, who could hardly wait to offer an experience he had while he was in Goa, India, when the statue visited. His eyes sparkled as he recalled in detail how Bishop Dom Jose Costa Nunes officiated with 153 priests celebrating the Holy Sacrifice of the Mass on 153 individual altars that were arranged in the form of a 15 decade Rosary—one altar for every bead of the Rosary—in an open air celebration. This was 1950—before Masses were concelebrated—and took place near the site of St. Francis Xavier's remains.

Personally, I witnessed the doves come upon the statue on May 2, 1978, in Rome. The story was related in the July/August issue of *Soul* magazine for 1982. The statue had been kept at the Shrine of Divina Amora (Divine Love), about ten miles from Rome, on May 1. At the offertory of the Mass, Fr. Pasquale Silla, rector of the sanctuary, placed two doves at the foot of the Pilgrim Virgin Statue and also released twenty more over the crowd. The two doves at the feet of the statue remained there all day.

The following day, at St. John Lateran Basilica, while preparing for Mass, three doves flew out of the sky, and headed straight for the feet of the statue. Efforts to dislodge them were unsuccessful.

Precisely at the Consecration, the doves flew up and perched on the arch above and to each side of the balcony. After communion they returned to Our Lady's feet, where they remained during the procession to St. Mary Major and through the night. The next day they were still there when the Statue was transported back to St. John Lateran for another Mass. Again at the Consecration they left, and this time flew to the column capitals next to the sanctuary. This time they stayed there, as the statue was being taken on a flight to Vienna.

In less than two weeks I witnessed the miracle again at Lourdes, France, as is mentioned in the chapter on the First World Pilgrimage. Three white doves landed on the red-carrier we use to house the statue while carrying it in procession. They remained ensconced at the feet of the image. When an unexpected light rain fell, I halted the four men carrying the statue, and removed her from the carrier. Upon doing so, the insides of my wrists brushed the immaculately white doves. Quickly I had Our Lady's image in the bus . . . the doves still remained in the carrier cooing for their Lady.

Through her image, Our Lady wishes to show us how serious our condition is by her tears, and how compassionately she longs for us to turn to her Divine Son. Then, the peace, love, and joy of the Holy Spirit, symbolized by the doves, will be able to settle upon the world.

IX.
Perfection

Tom Brown is an articulate, well loved and respected radio announcer for station KGIL, Los Angeles, California. Los Angeles had been suffering a terrible drought, one of the worst in decades. The day I arrived with Our Lady's image, October 1st, 1981, a torrential rain broke from the sky and graced the land, quenching the parched soil and relieving the anxiety of the people. On his broadcast that day, Tom Brown said, "Well, I guess L.A. is cleaning up its act, because Our Lady of Fatima will be here today at 12:00 noon on United Air lines!"

Clean up its act! In a few short words the radio announcer managed to state the central theme of Our Lady's message. "Men must reform their lives," she said. "Do not offend God Our Lord any more, for He is already deeply offended" (October 13, 1917).

Bishop Fulton J. Sheen said that God has two pictures of every one of us: a picture of what we are; and a picture of what we should be. He has but one picture of Mary, for She was both the ideal and the reality.

"You must be made perfect, as your heavenly Father is perfect" (Matthew 5:48). Christ's words are electrifying, a riddle. One can almost hear the faint, haunting murmur of the

Jews, laid to rest twenty centuries ago, saying, "This sort of talk is hard to endure! How can anyone take it seriously?" (John 6:60). But Pope Paul VI, in his Ash Wednesday, 1977, address warned "The World is under the power of Satan. We must do everything we can in our individual lives and through prayer to fight him."

With incomparable cunning, the devil tempts the human race today, as he did Adam and Eve. He offers evil in the guise of good; he covers sin with the coating of pleasure. He promises power and joy through the accumulation of unjust wealth, self sufficiency through pride. The world, the flesh and the devil create chaos continually, because the pleasures suggested leave the sinner with remorse of conscience, repugnance, and emptiness. Only after searching for happiness through pleasure, did St. Augustine realize that man was created for happiness, not pleasure: "Our hearts were created for thee, Lord, and they shall not rest until they rest in thee."

How Satan hates us! He tries unceasingly to guide us, through the world and the flesh, down the pathway to enter the "wide gate" that leads to destruction, in the company of many (Matthew 7:13-14), so that we may spend all eternity in the pits of his Hell in a furnace of fire where there shall be wailing and grinding of teeth (Matthew 13:42), and everlasting punishment (Matthew 25:46).

But how God loves us! He relentlessly showers us with His love and grace and leads us through prayer and penance up the pathway to enter the "narrow gate", which leads to life (Matthew 7:14). The Son of God, who is love, said, "I am indeed going to prepare a place for you, . . . that where I am you may also be" (John 14:3). God loves each one of us in a special way, as though we were the sole object of His infinite love. As Fr. Frederick Faber puts it:

> God does not look at us merely in the mass and multitude. As we shall stand single and alone before His judgment-seat, so do we stand, so have we always stood, single and alone before the eye of His boundless love. This is what each man

has to believe of himself. From all eternity God determined to create me . . . he resolved to create me such as I am, the me by which other people know me, a different me from any that have ever been created hitherto and from any that will be created hereafter. Un-numbered possible creatures, which God saw when He chose me, He left to remain in their nothingness. They might have worshipped Him a thousand times better than I shall ever worship Him. They might have been higher, holier and more interesting. But there was some nameless things about me which He preferred. His love fastened on something special in me. It was just me, with my individual peculiarities, the size, shape, fashion, and way of my particular, single, unmated soul, which in the calmness of his eternal predilection drew him to create me. I should not believe that God was God, if I did not believe this. This is the profession of faith which each of us should make in our hearts. I cannot tell how men endure life, who do not profess this faith in the Creator's special love.[1]

In creating us, and giving us a free will, God gave us three options: to be a saint; to be a devil; to be a fool. The saint will go to heaven; the devil to hell; the fool to purgatory. And it seems as though most will go to purgatory, for as the great William Shakespeare said, "What fools these mortals be."

Little Jacinta knew this well. Our Lady must have granted her a glimpse of life in eternity, for she would tell us in child-like simplicity "If people only knew what eternity is— what they would not do to change their lives."

Sanctity is so precious, it is worth paying any price to obtain it. No wonder Leon Bloy would exclaim "the saddest thing in the world is not to be a saint." Pope John XXIII, in his "Journey of a Soul" reveals "There is no way out. I must lead a hard, apostolic, crucified life. I must accustom myself to the love of suffering and self-denial." All of life should be a dress rehearsal for death.

Sanctity is possible for anyone to attain no matter what their calling in life. God sanctifies souls in the daily and hourly sacrifices required by their station in life. God does not expect us to punish our bodies, to crucify our flesh, in order to become saints. But sweetly He would lead us to holiness by our constant faithfulness to our daily duty, duty accepted, duty done for His sake: "To endure is to adore. You will become a saint by complying exactly with your daily duties" (Saint Mary Joseph Rosell).

Our journey through life is an interior one—spiritual—in which we never stay on the same plateau. We either progress or retrogress. By joyfully embracing the many little hard and painful things which come to us each hour we come closer to Christ until one day we begin to think like Christ, talk like Christ, act like Christ, pray like Christ, love like Christ, become another Christ!

We are all auditioning for an everlasting role in Heaven. God is the auditioner; Our Lady our constant, faithful coach. "Do whatever he tells you" were her words of advice at Cana in the first century; "Penance, penance, penance," at Lourdes in February of 1858; "I have come to warn the faithful to amend their lives and ask pardon for their sins. They must not continue to offend Our Lord, Who is already deeply offended," at Fatima in October of 1917. To pass the test we have to comply with the requests of Our Lady—which is conformity to the will of God.

The more we submit to the Divine Will the more we advance. St. Teresa said to her spiritual daughters,

> Direct your prayer to the one thing only; that is, to conform your will perfectly to the Divine Will. Be assured that there is no greater perfection attainable than this conformity, and that they who most earnestly strive for it will receive from God the richest graces and most quickly advance in the interior life. Believe me, this is the secret. Upon this point alone rests our sanctification.

The air smelled of sunlight and grass as Fr. Aloysius Bartko's lawn was being mowed at Christ the King Church, Akron,

Ohio. Spending some time in a relaxing conversation with him, I asked his definition of a saint. He replied, "I like the late Fr. Daniel Lord's answer to that question, 'A saint is a person who at all times and in all circumstances does what he or she thinks is the Holy will of God.' "

All unhappiness is caused from wanting our will. "Happiness is wanting what you have; not having what you want." Accepting God's will is the only real source of peace and happiness. The souls in Hell are there because they did their will, not God's. With great remorse do they now realize that time was given them in this life to purchase eternity by faithfully fulfilling God's will.

The holy man of Dublin, Matt Talbot, was so conscious of God's will and Our Lady's powerful intercession that he wrote in one of his many books, "Three things I cannot escape: the eye of God, the voice of conscience, the stroke of death."[2] In another book he wrote, "Oh, Virgin, three things I beg of you: the grace of God, the presence of God, the Benediction of God."[3]

"The saints are the spiritual geniuses," Francis Thompson told us, for they had the presence of mind to realize there is but one heartbeat between them and death, that the greatest teacher is Professor Death, that the greatest school is the cemetery.

It is well to remember the Parable of the rich man, as St. Luke tells us:

> There was a rich man who had a good harvest. "What shall I do?" he asked himself. "I have no place to store my harvest. I know!" he said, "I will pull down my grain bins and build larger ones. All my grain and my goods will go there. Then I will say to myself: You have blessings in reserve for years to come. Relax! Eat heartily, drink well. Enjoy yourself." But God said to him, "You fool! This very night your life shall be required of you. To whom will all this piled up wealth of yours go?" That is the way it works with the man who grows rich for himself instead of growing rich in the sight of God. (Luke 12:16-21)

Life is short; eternity forever! God wants us to live our lives to the fullest. Nothing can happen to us that He does not allow or cause. God gave everyone a select cross which He blessed lovingly from all eternity. He wants us to carry it with resignation. "If a man wishes to come after me he must deny his very self, take up his cross and begin to follow in my footsteps" (Matthew 16:24).

In the second apparition of the Angel, the Summer of 1916, the angel emphatically told the three Fatima Children, "Above all, accept and bear with submission the sufferings that the Lord may send you."[4]

St. Maximilian Kolbe, canonized by Pope John Paul II, used to walk to the blackboard at Niepokolanow (a city in Poland, 25 miles west of Warsaw, which he founded and named). In English it means "City of the Immaculate Conception". There he would write on the board for his Franciscan seminarians, "The formula for sanctity is: w = W." The little "w" represents our will, the capital "W" God's.

> The crowd seated around him told him, "Your mother and your brothers and sisters are outside asking for you." He said in reply, "Who are my mother and my brothers?" And gazing around him at those seated in the circle he continued, "These are my mother and my brothers. Whoever does the will of God is brother and sister and mother to me." (Mark 3:32-33)

Jesus does not disclaim the bonds of physical relationship with his mother, but he seizes the opportunity to give a lesson on the greater dignity of spiritual relationship. St. Augustine says that Mary was more blessed in that she believed in Christ than in that she had given him birth.[5] Dan Lyons says:

> What He [God] mainly asks of anyone is that he fulfill the duties of his state of life. For most people that means raising and supporting a family, and keeping the Commandments. I like to think of St. Joseph, who spent most of his life at his

job. He was a bread-winner and a family man, yet he is rated above all the saints who have succeeded him.[6]

Loving God with all our heart, soul, strength and will—and our neighbor as ourself—will bring us to perfection as we perform our daily obligations. In Fr. Clarke's words,

> The highest and most perfect kind of life does not consist in one occupation more than another, not in severe penances, not in active zeal, not in works of self-denying charity, not in living remote from all in order to spend one's life in contemplation and prayer, but simply in doing the will of God from day to day.[7]

Alexandrina da Costa, during the last thirteen and one half years of her life, ate and drank nothing but the Eucharist, which she received with moving devotion every morning. [8]

In the hushed stillness of her room, on the very day she would die, October 13, 1955, she gave a last piercing message to all mankind in this perilous nuclear age: "Do not sin; the pleasures of this life are worth nothing. Receive Communion, pray the Rosary every day. This sums up everything."[9]

Tradition tells us Our Lady made her first apparition to our Earth in the first century, appearing on top of a pillar at Saragosa, Spain, on the shore of the Ebro River.[10] Her last apparition to our Earth, currently approved by Holy Mother the Church, took place on March 2, 1933, when she showed herself in Belgium to a fourteen-year-old girl, Mariette Beco.[11] In between the first and the last, she has made numerous apparitions. A very striking one occurred on September 19, 1846, when she appeared in Southern France, at La Salette, to the children Maximin Giraud, eleven years of age, and Melanie Mathieu, fifteen years of age:

> The first thing the children saw was a globe of dazzling light. While they gazed in wonderment, the globe opened

and they saw a woman seated on some stones which surrounded the bed of a spring. The spring was dry at the time.
The Lady's elbows rested on her knees, her face was buried
in her hands, and she was weeping. [12]

It is the only time in all of her apparitions that the Mother of
God cried! She shed tears because people will not stop offending God by sin.

"You can't offend God by sin," some would have us believe.
When Christ took the whip to the money changers in the
temple, did he do so because they were offending man by sin;
or did he do so because they were offending God by sin? Our
Lady's Fatima message has taken away any doubt.

One sin cast Lucifer and his minions into Eternal fire; one
sin cost man Paradise; one sin required that the Son of God die
for us on the cross to redeem us.

Pope Paul VI said that, "What the Church needs today is
'saints,' men and women whose lives faithfully reflect the
intrinsic sanctity that is an essential property of the Church of
Christ." He urged the faithful to mirror this sanctity in their
daily lives. "The sanctity which is required of us is not the one
of miracles, but of good and strong will. It is this Christian
witness the Church so desperately needs today." [13]

John Cardinal Henry Newman tells how to obtain the
sanctity of "good and strong will".

Do not lie in bed beyond the due time of rising; give your
first thoughts to God; make a good visit to the Blessed
Sacrament; say the Angelus devoutly; eat and drink to God's
glory; say the Rosary well; be recollected; keep out bad
thoughts; make your evening meditation well; examine
yourself daily; go to bed in good time; and—YOU ARE
ALREADY PERFECT.

Love is at the basis of perfection. St John of God said, "Do
all the good you can, to all the people that you can, at all the

times that you can, in all the places that you can, in all the ways that you can, as long as you can." His contemporary, the great St John of the Cross, the Doctor of Mystical Theology, reiterates this: "In the twilight of our lives we shall be judged on how we loved." St. Augustine tells us to "Love God, and do what you will." If we love God we will do His will.

The food of Love is the Eucharist. Daily, millions of Catholics nourish themselves with the food of everlasting life from the Son of God in the Eucharist—the center and crux of the Catholic Faith. Our Lady made her first appearance at Fatima on May 13, 1917, which is the feast day of, "Our Lady of the Blessed Sacrament."

Christ gave Peter the keys to the Kingdom of Heaven (Matthew 16:19). Peter gives us the key to our riddle. He hurled defiance at nature when, at the gentle beckoning of the God-Savior, he dared to walk on the water. He continued in this inconceivable, stupendous feat as long as he kept his eyes on Christ! Perfection is possible as long as we keep our eyes on Jesus.

Sin brings death, not life. Our drug-ridden, promiscuous, heartsick society has anesthetized millions. God knows the innumerable army of souls trekking life's road in a quandary, seeking happiness but not knowing where to find it. Repentance is the answer—not something of gloom and despair, but a life giving response to God's Love.

We need to persevere in our goal to strive for perfection. In Dom Hubert Van Zeller's words,

> The Church says that when anyone perseveres in his God-given state of life without rebellion, self-pity, escape, eccentricity, fussiness, vanity or a desire to attract personal attention, this can only mean that God's grace is at work in the soul to an extraordinary degree.[14]

Many in our power-hungry world are possessed by Satan or obsessed with him. We need souls who are possessed by Christ!

Ejaculation for Perfection

Oh Mary, through your Immaculate Conception, cleanse my body and sanctify my soul.

Prayer for Perfection

Oh God, infinite holiness, goodness and perfection, lead me to sanctity. Increase and refine my love. Turn it into a burning, leaping flame—a fiery furnace of love. Raise me above my mundane self. Do for me what I am unable to do for myself. Drown my pride, my selfishness and attachments in the abyss of thy love and humility of thy Sacred Heart.

NOTES

[1]Fr. Faber, Frederick Wm., D. P., *Spiritual Conference*, Tan Books Publishers, Inc., Rockford, Ill., 61105, pp. 327-328.

[2]Purcell, Mary, *The Life and Times of Matt Talbot*, Newman Press, Westminster, Md., p. 110.

[3]*Ibid.*, p. 153.

[4]De Marchi, John, *Mother of Christ Crusade*, Billings, Montana, 59105, p. 7.

[5]*De Virginibus*, p. 111.

[6]McCallum, John D., *The Story of Dan Lyons*, Guild Books, 86 Riverside Dr., N.Y., N.Y., 10024, p. 196.

[7]Clarke, S.J., *The Secret of Perfection*, Daughters of St. Paul, Boston, Mass., 02130, holy card.

[8]Johnson, Francis, *The Miracle of Alexandrina*, The Blue Army, Washington, N.J., 07882, p. 12.

[9]*Ibid.*, p. 15.

[10]Sister Lamberty, Manetta, S.C.C., *The Woman in Orbit*, The Lamberty Co., Inc., 325 W. Huron St., Chicago, Ill., 60610, p. 8.

[11]Sharkey, Don, *The Woman Shall Conquer*, Franciscan Mary-

town Press, Kenosha, Wisc., 53140, p. 135.

[12]*Ibid.*, p. 35.

[13]Vatican City (RNS), "Summer Address to a general audience," 1976.

[14]Van Zeller, Dom Hubert, *Sanctity in Other Words*, Templegate, Springfield, Ill., p. 85.

X.
Hail, Holy Queen

I have been privileged to escort for many years, both nationally and internationally, the material vehicle through which God makes manifest countless miracles—many in the realm of nature, a veritable deluge in the realm of grace—the International Pilgrim Virgin Statue of Our Lady of the Rosary, familiarly known as Our Lady of Fatima. Surely the finger of God touched the man who sculpted this wondrous image of the Mother of God.

The story began in 1917, as the guns of war rumbled and reverberated across Europe. White sands blotted the red blood of dead and wounded soldiers. Young mothers wept in the dark of night. Old men stared. Death and destruction reigned.

Jose Thedim, a Portuguese sculptor, on the thirteenth day of October, 1917, saw the sun dance in the sky and then plunge earthward; he was present at the "Miracle of the Sun." He returned to his father's house, and with St. Joseph as his patron, began his life's work. Partly from his own imagination, and partly from written instructions from Lucia, he carved a Statue of Our Lady of the Rosary of Fatima for the Bishop of Leiria, Fatima diocese.

123

The statue was to be installed in its place of honor at the shrine on May 13, 1920. The powers of darkness were at work behind the scenes. The revolutionary government of Portugal meant to put an end once and for all, to the "foolishness of Fatima." The impetus for such action had been gathering force. The secular press continuously ridiculed the event, claiming that it was a plot to restore the Church to the prestige she enjoyed before the revolution. The early deaths of Francisco, on April 4, 1919, and of Jacinta, on February 20, 1920, gave rise to the story that the Jesuits had murdered the two, and that Lucy was putty in the hands of these evil clerics.[1]

Word of the miracle had spread like brush fire through Portugal's towns, cities and countryside. The government propaganda could not extinguish the fires of faith. Seventy thousand people viewed the Miracle of the Sun at the Cova: thousands more within a twenty-five mile radius of the Cova also saw the miracle. The revolutionaries could not rewrite reality. The Catholic Press was cautious. Some priests, intimidated by the political situation, strongly condemned the seers. The Patriarch of Lisbon threatened to excommunicate any priest who promoted the Fatima devotion. But the people knew the Mother of God heard their prayers at Fatima. They had seen the dying restored to life, the lame walk, and the blind see.

In the early hours of the morning on the 13th of May, 1920, many were on their way to Fatima to enshrine their Mother's image. Like a small army, they trudged the roads and lanes leading to the Cova. From time to time a fine carriage pulled by sleek horses scattered the crowds. Great rolls of dust billowed across the fields.

When the crowds reached their destination, they found two regiments of the Portuguese army encircling the hallowed ground. Rifles and bayonets glistened in the light. The government planned to stop the display of faith by force. Perhaps on that day Jose Thedim was there, and prayed to his patron St.

Joseph to protect the people and the work of his hands from the power of evil; for, undaunted and confident, Mary's little army stormed Heaven with their weapon—the rosary. Like the Welch miners of old, they sang to her loud and fervently. Their enemies were not destroyed but reborn in faith. The soldiers forgot their guns, their government, and joined in the chorus. The image of Our Lady was carried aloft to its place of honor accompanied by shouts of joy. Today, that first image from the hands of Jose Thedim still stands in the Chapel of the Apparitions.

The revolutionaries continued their campaign to discredit Fatima. In 1922, the little chapel was destroyed by bombs, though the altar, shrine and Our Lady's image were untouched.[2] To make reparation for the desecration of the holy ground, some sixty thousand believers assembled on May 13th, the same year.

In 1926, the government, which had ridiculed and persecuted the Fatima Pilgrims, was toppled by three generals, and Salazar came to power. In 1927, the Bishop of Fatima presided over a pilgrimage for the first time. The following year, he welcomed 300,000 pilgrims in one day.

The canonical investigations concerning Fatima, begun in 1922, were completed eight years later. The apparitions were declared worthy of belief. The following year, the Bishop of Fatima, together with the entire hierarchy of his country, solemnly consecrated Portugal to the Immaculate Heart of Mary.

In 1936, the forces that evoked the Spanish Civil War were threatening Portugal's borders. Because of this danger, the bishops gathered at the Cova da Iria in May 1936, to rededicate their land to Mary. They pledged that if Our Lady protected Portugal from war and red revolution, they would return in public thanksgiving. In 1938, they returned rejoicing, with their flocks numbering half a million.

It came as no surprise to Jose Thedim to hear that his

countrymen at the Portuguese College in Rome wanted him to re-create Her image. Was this the sign of Mary reaching out through the work of his hands to spread her message? He must have labored with great love and devotion, for his second creation was one of exquisite beauty. Pope Pius XII, upon viewing the statue, was so overwhelmed that he summoned its maker to the Vatican. Did Jose Thedim give thanks to the good God for his talent on that long trip to Rome? He must have thought a good deal about his patron St. Joseph. Did he wonder if his clothing were suitable? Did he wonder where he would stay? He must have prayed the rosary and had long thoughts about the mystery of it all. He, Jose Thedim, at the Vatican! His Holiness invested Thedim with the "Croce Pro Ecclesia and Pontifice" and bestowed upon him the title "Comendador." Our Lady must have smiled upon this meeting of the Vicar of her Son with her humble workman from the mountain country. Upon his return to his village, his neighbors were, no doubt, awestruck and likely wondered if he would move away to some grander place.

On the 25th anniversary of the apparitions, Pope Pius XII telegraphed his blessings to the Fatima pilgrims and to Portugal. The same year in Rome, in the presence of some 40,000 people, he consecrated the entire world to the Immaculate Heart of Mary. Our Lady of Fatima had burst the boundaries of Portugal.[3]

In the same year, 1942, for the first time the statue journeyed from the shrine to Lisbon for a Catholic Youth Congress. There was an outpouring of faith as the Queen of Heaven, through her Son, dispensed grace to the unbelieving. There were numerous conversions.

Four years later, Our Lady's image left the shrine again to visit Lisbon. A great sea of humanity awaited her arrival. As she was carried into the crowd, snow-white doves flew to the base of the statue and remained there motionless. The grace of repentance flooded the city and countless sinners were washed clean through the sacrament of penance. Rejoicing crowds followed Our Lady's image as she was carried through the city in triumph. The bands played; the people sang to the lowly Jewish maiden God made His mother. The white doves nestled at her feet oblivious to the crowds, the music and the motion, until her image was finally back in the country of the shepherds. What signs of wonder and mystery in God's creation!

War battered the borders of the land of Mary, but her people held fast to the Rosary. Their mother sheltered and protected them. And then came the great day; World War II was over. The women of Portugal gathered their jewels—diamonds, rubies, emeralds, pearls and thousands of precious stones—and made from them a crown of thanksgiving,[4] their gift to the Mother of God for her gift to them, the jewel of peace. The rich, the poor, the lame and the halt in a crowd of 700,000 came with grateful hearts to her shrine. On that day of public thanksgiving, May 13, 1946, the legate of Pope Pius XII, in company with the hierarchy and clergy, solemnly crowned Our Lady of Fatima Queen of Peace. The voice of the Pontiff from Rome was heard in the Cova:

> And the King saw that she was truly worthy of such honor . . .because [she was] more filled with grace, more holy, more beautiful . . . she is the first born daughter of the Father, pure Mother of the Word, beloved bride of the Holy Ghost . . . you have bound yourselves . . . to imitate her so that with her blessing you may better serve the Divine King. . . .
>
> So the Church salutes her Lady and Queen of Angels . . . ; she acclaims her Queen of Heaven and earth . . . Queen of the Universe. . . .[5]

Jose Thedim must have witnessed the work of his hands adorned with the jewels of Portugal, and knew he had only begun. The Bishop of Leiria requested another image of Our Lady of the Rosary of Fatima.

Being a practical country man, Jose Thedim decided the

best way to set about his new creation was to visit Sister Lucy and ask for information, for she had seen the Mother of God. Having prayed and pondered, and armed with a long list of written questions, as well as the permission of his bishop, he met Sister Lucy for the first time November 9, 1946.[6]

He must have felt some misgivings at her description of the Queen of Heaven:

> . . . we beheld a Lady all dressed in white. She was more brilliant than the sun and radiated a light more clear and intense than a crystal glass filled with sparkling water when the rays of the burning sun shine through it. She seemed to be made all of light and her garments also.

Pure light. How could he carve such a figure? The woman of the Apocalypse—a woman clothed with the sun! No, he could not make such a likeness; nor, for that matter, could anyone else. He made a series of sketches and returned to the convent for Lucy's approval. He then made a plaster cast and made a third trip to the convent; again Lucy approved. Jose Thedim then set about to carve the image in wood, and from that wood emerged the world-famous International Pilgrim Virgin Statue of Our lady of the Rosary of Fatima.[8]

On May 13, 1947, the good and kindly Bishop of Fatima blessed this image, and with the approbation of Sister Lucy gave it into the care of the Catholic Youth Congress. The Mother of God, through this image, set out on her pilgrimage. For her Divine Son she would gather the lost souls of broken Europe. From country to country she journeyed; from city to city; from church to church; and everywhere masses of people reached out. The signs and wonders accompanying her visitations caused Pope Pius XII to exclaim, "As she sets forth to claim her dominions, the miracles she performs along the way are such that we can scarcely believe our eyes. . . ."[9]

Souls, dried and parched from the fires of war, were washed with the living waters of God's grace. Through her intercession, God healed the sick and gave sight to the blind. Her children kissed the feet of the symbol of their Mother in Heaven and wept. They wept for the scourge of evil they had endured, evil wrought by sin, evil that brought down the innocent with the guilty. Mary must have wept with them and remembered when she fled into Egypt with Joseph, remembering the taste of her tears for Rachel bewailing her children, because they were not. Mary came to her people in compassion, in pity, and warning. Compassion wedded to admonition: "Go and sin no more."

Jose Thedim may have walked to his village to get a newspaper in order to follow the accounts of this miraculous image. Likely he talked to St. Joseph about them, and prayed that the souls of men would be truly renewed, and that they would find a lasting peace here and hereafter.

What was he thinking as he worked on two new images of Our Lady of Fatima? Did the Bishop tell him their destination? Was he surprised that day, when the dew was on the grass and the pines scented the air with their sweetness, that the International Pilgrim Virgin returned for a time to visit him? The devotion of the faithful had worn out her left foot with their veneration. With slow patience he carved an exact duplicate from ivory and then bid farewell to his creation. The daughter of Jose Thedim, Maria Theresa, has given me this wooden relic of the miraculous statue—this relic worn with the love of the victims of war. For her kindness and generosity, may the angels smooth her path!

On October 13, 1947, a second International Pilgrim Virgin Statue was blessed. The Bishop of Leiria-Fatima, conducting the ceremonies in the presence of 200,000 people, six bishops, and many dignitaries, did not crown the statue, but commented that the crowning would be done later, on American soil.[10]

When I became the escort of the Pilgrim Virgin, on September 2, 1975, I was given charge of the first, or "European"

Statue, that had been blessed on May 13, 1947. Then, on September 2, 1982, the first statue was returned to Fatima to remain there permanently, and I was given charge of the second, or "American" statue. I can testify that *both* statues have been the instruments of the wonders that have been performed along the way.

NOTES

[1]Walsh, Wm. Thomas, *Our Lady of Fatima*, Image Books, A Division of Doubleday & Co., Inc., Garden City, New York, 1954, pp. 183, 184.

[2]*Ibid.*, p. 204.

[3]Johnson, Francis, *Fatima, the Great Sign*, Tan Books & Publishers, Inc., 1980, p. 11.

[4]*Ibid.*, pp. 124, 125.

[5]Walsh, Wm. Thomas, *Op. Cit.*, pp. 214, 215.

[6]Thedim, Maria Theresa, Porto, Portugal, letter to Edward Moran, dtd February 20, 1983.

[7]Johnson, Francis, *Op. Cit.*, pp. 27, 28.

[8]Thedim, M. T., *Op. Cit.*, (1 tr).

[9]Johnson, Francis, *Op. Cit.*, p. 125.

[10]Haffert, John, *Russia Will be Converted*, AMI Press, Washington, New Jersey, c. 1956, Chapter 14.

XI.
1983 World Pilgrimage

For ten years I have been honored, privileged and tremendously blessed as I have escorted Our Lady's famed statue over one million miles around the world, on both sides of the Iron Curtain. When not on a world pilgrimage, the statue is generally booked for a month at a time in a United States Diocese. The mode of transportation is usually by plane, with the statue occupying a window seat, and myself sitting alongside. The statue travels at a child's fare, half price. I fasten a safety-belt around the statue, and in minutes, the famed image of the Blessed Virgin is off into the wide blue sky, offering to assist us in chasing away all blues by living her program of peace, joy and hope for the world.

In December of 1983, I accompanied the International Statue around the world on a most rigorous, challenging pilgrimage: 40,000 miles in 19 days! It was a demanding, hectic pace. In circling the earth, we averaged over 2,000 miles per day—a whirlwind stint—spending 65 hours of flying time in commercial 747 Jumbo-Jets.

On a bright, brisk December 4th morning, I carried Our Lady's image on board the jet plane at Bishop Airport, Flint, Michigan, where our pilgrimage originated with connecting flights in Chicago and San Francisco. We left the United States on Quantas Airlines and arrived in Sydney, Australia—the country on the underside of the world. Sydney is a thriving, bustling city, populated with three million inhabitants, who are very interested in current events. Upon our touching down at the airport, after a twelve hour flight, the news media promptly went to work. Within hours invitations were extended to appear on four television stations and to do three radio interviews. The newspaper coverage was excellent, giving Our Lady's visitation great impetus. The first proof was the tremendous crowd that had gathered at St. Mary's Cathedral; over 6,000! The excitement was high, almost to a fever pitch. At a given signal from an usher, the statue was lifted into the air upon the shoulders of two priests and two laymen, and carried very proudly by the bearers to the accompaniment of the lovely organ and choir singing "Immaculate Mary." You could feel the grace being showered; it was evident on every face! The emotions were mixed: awed silence; copious tears; radiant smiles; mesmerized eyes. With the statue enthroned in the sanctuary, Archbishop Clancy celebrated the Holy Sacrifice of the Mass for world peace.

During the recessional, walking directly behind the statue, I momentarily lapsed back in time to the Annual National Sacred Heart Conference held in the United States on August 25, 1980, at the Immaculate Conception Cathedral in Washington, D.C.. Carrying the International statue, in another solemn procession, were some of the outstanding churchmen of our day: John Cardinal Carberry; Maurice Cardinal Otunga, Archbishop of Nairobi, Kenya, Africa; Most Rev. Peter Canisius Van Lierde, Vicar General of Pope John Paul II; and the Most Rev. Thomas J. Welsh, Bishop of Arlington, Virginia.

From the cathedral, we traveled to other churches where the same fervor was apparent in the crowds. Inevitably, one could detect the quivering of voices as they sang "Immaculate Mary" while the image processed down the center aisles.

Hands or handkerchiefs were used slowly or quickly to wisk away the unrestrained tears. It was a most touching scene.

From Sydney we flew to beautiful Melbourne for a two day visitation with the same warmth and welcome we received in Sydney. Three churches received the Pilgrim Statue enthusiastically.

We were in the air again, flying some 2,200 miles from Melbourne to Perth (called the most isolated large city in the world because of its location). On the long flight, a doctor sat next to me. He was amiable and quite young. In a jovial mood he asked me, "Would you like me to give her a check-up?" "No, Doc," I answered, "She is here to give *you* a check-up." Laughter broke out in the immediate area and was contagious!

Landing in Perth, we saw an enormous cavalcade of cars waiting to wisk Our Lady's image off to the various churches. (I have to admit, however, it wasn't the largest cavalcade I have ever witnessed. That was in the Cincinnati Diocese of Ohio: 305 automobiles escorted by state police from Kentucky and Ohio.

Susanne Roberts, writer for the "West Australian" newspaper, wrote on December 12, 1983: "A station wagon covered with thousands of red and white carnations yesterday carried one of the most famous religious objects, the International Pilgrim Statue of Our Lady of Fatima, from Perth airport. Over 500 people were at the airport to pay homage."

As the flower-covered station wagon, with the statue mounted securely on top wended its way through the streets of Perth, escorted by two police officers riding Harley-Davidson motorcycles, people walking the streets would pause, bow, and continue on their way. Some would make the sign of the cross or genuflect on the sidewalks, as they took note of this auspicious and rare event.

An enormous crowd came to venerate the statue in St. Patrick's Church, Freemantle. After the services, a little cherub—a blonde, blue-eyed girl, four years of age, being held by her mother's hand—stood watching intently with hundreds of people as I dismantled the statue and was about to place her in her blue traveling bag. Suddenly she cried out, "Mommy, don't let him put Our Lady in that bag!"

St. Mary's Cathedral had the biggest crowd it had ever seen when Our Lady's image was there. Over twenty priests were present, and a number commented they had never seen a larger turn-out. Solemn Mass was followed by an all-night vigil, with crowds pouring in at all hours of the night.

We flew to the Island of Tasmania, just south of Australia. We took Our Lady's image to the "Church of the Apostles" in Launcistown, where throngs poured into the church. The Church, like the island, captures your imagination as you survey its beauty. You have to look several times, thinking you might have missed something the first time. You have the feeling that you are in another place, another time.

Next we were off to Harare, Zimbabwe, Africa, which was formerly known as Salisbury, Rhodesia, before falling to the atheistic communists. The flight took ten hours. Our Lady's statue was tucked securely into the seat on the port side of the plane, while I was sitting next to her. In no time we reached an altitude of 37,000 feet above the Indian Ocean. The clouds were large and billowy. We were cruising at 575 miles per hour. I looked out the window and was almost blinded by the intensity of the brilliant sun. Thoughts flashed through my mind . . . "Light is God's first creature," (Francis Bacon); "God's eldest daughter," (Thomas Fuller); "Offspring of Heaven's firstborn," (Milton); "The first of painters," (Emerson); "You can't see light but you can see with it," (C. S. Lewis); "Light is the shadow of God," (Plato) . . . my eyelids became heavy, and I fell into a welcome sleep.

The wonderful fragrance of freshly brewed coffee struck my nostrils and roused me from sleep. The stewardesses were preparing a treat of coffee and cake. A father was escorting his young son, holding a Linus-blanket in one hand and a Snoopy dog in the other, to the restroom. On his way back his curiosity got the better of him, and he asked, jokingly, "Got a bomb in that bag?" "Yep, a spiritual bomb that can shake-up the whole world!"

The stewardess that served me asked if she could sit in the vacant seat across the aisle and ask some questions. I nodded my head. We discussed the statue, the tears, the doves, and the purpose of its travels. She was searching for answers. Her final question was, "How can you be so sure you have an immortal soul?" I related the story St. Augustine told of Genadius, who also had that question. He was praying continuously that God would solve his dilemma. One day God sent an Angel to the foot of his bed, while he was fast asleep. The Angel asked, "Genadius, do you hear me?" "Yes, I hear you." "Do you hear me with your ears?" "No, I'm fast asleep. I do not know what I hear you with." "Genadius, do you see me?" "Yes I do see you." "Do you see me with your eyes?" "No, I am fast asleep. I do not know what I see you with." "Genadius, are you speaking to me?" "Yes, I am speaking to you." "Are you speaking to me with your mouth?" "No my mouth is closed, I do not know what I am speaking to you with." "Genadius, you heard me, you saw me, and you spoke to me with your immortal soul."

Soon it was time for viewing movies on the giant airplane. Three different movies were generally shown in three different sections of the plane. A delicious meal followed. In a few minutes we were snoozing again.

At 11:05 p.m., we landed at Harare. I was astonished to see a huge cavalcade of cars waiting to take us to the Immaculate Conception Church at this hour of the night. A brand new Mercedes-Benz car was outfitted to accommodate the statue on the roof, with spotlights shining brightly on her. We drove eleven miles from the airport to the church, following the winding roads. We arrived at 12:30 a.m., to see a standing-room-only crowd cheering, as Our Lady processed into the sanctuary. After the enthronement, a tumultuous clapping of the hands thundered throughout the church, as the people showed Our Lady their great love for her, as represented by this famous image. I was one of the four white people present. At least 1,000 black people were there to pay homage. Their faith is alive, dynamic! They truly prayed the rosary devoutly, pronouncing every word distinctly, and in a chanting fashion.

Entering this communist country (Zimbabwe) was no problem; but leaving it was like a fly trying to escape a spider's web! After a much needed sleep, I was taken to the airport. The guards were bearing arms, as they do in all communist countries. I was given the "third degree." My luggage was searched very carefully; the statue received an even closer examination, being tapped gently for hollow spots, which might be secret compartments for contraband. I was asked to spread my legs apart, and raise my arms high in the air, while they frisked me convict-style. They demanded my wallet, insisting I pay them to leave the country—$100.00 would do nicely! We bickered back and forth. All the while, they were becoming more adamant. I was told, in no uncertain terms, they could hold me in the country if I didn't comply with their wishes. This was Czechoslovakia all over! The guards were gruff. I honestly thought I would not get out of their country, for I had previously been warned of tourists who were deliberately kept in jail for endless months for the most unbelievable reasons.

My concern could not have been greater when, out of nowhere, a Catholic priest came to my rescue and dished out a good tongue lashing to the guards for their treatment of me. Strangely, the guards said nothing. I was wondering if this was St. John the Baptist, or St. John the Evangelist . . . maybe even St. Joseph? The priest disappeared almost like a vapor as I ran, statue in arms, to catch the plane which was already winding up its engines. As in Czechoslovakia, I was happy to shake the dust from my shoes upon leaving Zimbabwe. Soon we were airborne. The two hour flight to Johannesburg, South Africa, was filled with prayers for the captive people in the communists nations, with intermittent thoughts of that priest who had rescued me. Surely, Our Lady had sent him.

We went to several churches in Johannesburg. At St. Francis of Assisi in Yeoville, the priest in charge wanted permission for the people to ask questions after the service. The questions revealed there was a deep hunger for devotion to the Mother of God.

Into the air again, we were flying to Durban to visit three churches. All-night vigils were held with packed churches. Archbishop Hurley requested my presence. He wanted to ask questions. Meeting his excellency, I was impressed by his kindness and patience. "How is the Blue Army being accepted through the world?" was one of the first questions he fired at me. "Beautifully, your excellency," I responded, and then I elaborated. "What is the Blue Army doing in the United States?" I mentioned the cell hours of holiness, the First Five Saturday programs being promoted, the travels of both the National and the International Pilgrim Virgin Statues, the movie we are in the progress of making, the slide-programs, cadet-programs, and so on. "What do you think of South Africa?" "I love it. It is not what I anticipated—it is so modern!" After a lengthy conversation, we said good-bye. He told me I was always welcome to come back.

In the air again: Cape Town. At the huge cathedral we had an all night vigil with adoration of the Blessed Sacrament and veneration of the statue. Many were those who sacrificed sleep to spend holy moments before the Eucharist: God's supreme proof of love for man—Heaven in our midst.

In my wallet is a 3x5 index card, folded, which I have carried for over 20 years. It's a saying by the Jesuit, Father Willie Doyle, which I typed and which has always borne fruit for me,

> Real devotion to the Blessed Sacrament is only to be gained by hard, grinding work of dry adoration before the hidden God. But such a treasure cannot be purchased at too

great a cost, for once obtained, it makes of this life as near an approach to heaven as we can ever hope for.

Well would St. Augustine say, "God in his omnipotence could not give more, in His wisdom He knew not how to give more, in His riches He had not more to give, than the Eucharist."

Francis Thompson, too, would trigger our awareness of His Real Presence, "The day is a priest and each morning the priest goes to the Orient Tabernacle; lifts from out of it the host; raises it in Benediction over the world and sets it at night in the flaming monstrance of the West."

I stared in wonder at the host in the monstrance—the bread of life—praying three times the prayer the Angel taught the three children to pray: "My God, I believe, I adore, I hope, and I love you; I beg pardon of You for those who do not believe, do not adore, do not hope and do not love you."

It seemed only natural to ponder the concluding scene of Our Lady's first apparition, on May 13, 1917, to the same three children when She asked them, "Do you want to offer yourselves to God to endure all the sufferings that He may choose to send you, as an act of reparation for the sins by which He is offended and as a supplication for the conversion of sinners?"

Promptly Lucia replied for all three, "Yes." As she pronounced these words, Our Lady opened her hands and shed upon the children a highly intense light. Lucia said the light penetrated them to the heart and allowed them to see themselves in God, Who was that light. Then they were moved by an inward impulse to fall on their knees while repeating, "Most Holy Trinity, I adore you! My God, my God, I love you in the Blessed Sacrament."

At one of the churches we visited, not far from the cathedral, a young man with a ruddy complexion excitedly told me that he and sixteen of his Protestant family members became

Catholic because of the Blessed Virgin Mary and her statue! I prodded him with questions. Most graciously he answered, beaming all the while with an inner joy that could not be contained. He said, "I heard a cassette tape on the International Pilgrim Virgin's 1978 World tour and that was the grace I needed to convert. I challenged the members of my family to listen to the tape and they too received the grace of conversion."

Cardinal Owen McGann extended an invitation to me through the coordinator. After a gentle rap on the door, his secretary greeted us warmly, asking us to be seated in very comfortable chairs. In two minutes the aging Cardinal was shaking our hands. He was spry, witty and inquisitive. "How long have you traveled with the statue? How many countries have you been to? What kind of a reception did you receive in Poland? What is it like to travel behind the Iron Curtain?" As I answered these questions the Cardinal seemed to be lost in thought, deep thought. Another series of questions were put forth with the final one being, "When do you foresee the triumph of the Immaculate Heart?" With my answer, "Only God knows," we ended the conversation. The Cardinal most graciously thanked me for bringing the statue to his Archdiocese, inviting a return whenever possible.

We left Cape Town making a refueling stop at the Cape Verde Island, a Portuguese owned province, before flying up to London, England, where I would board a Northwest Orient 747 for the U.S.A.

Sitting in the lobby at Heathrow Airport on December 23rd, I purchased a London Times Newspaper while waiting to board my flight. I was stunned, reading an article that said they were closing down an average of 65 churches a year in London alone. The reasons for the closings were high taxes, loss of faith, affluence, and a general decline of religion. What were they using the buildings for? Grocery stores, mortuaries, antique shops, hardwares, devil worship, and prostitution.

Fr. Paul Marx, O.S.B., in his "Human Life International," report No. 11, page 1, said "John Paul II lamented the French Canadians' plunge in Mass attendance from 90% when he visited Canada 15 years ago to only 15% today." And on page 5, "Less than 3% in any Scandinavian country still attend church. . . . The Dutch Church makes Canada's seem downright healthy. Only about 10% of the people and the priests believe. . . . Out of 36 million baptized Anglicans, only 750,000 still go to church on Sunday in England." On page 6, "Nationally, only 17% of Catholics [in Germany] go to church; in Catholic Munich, less than 10%."

A coordinator for a diocese in the U.S. who spent many years in France working for the U.S. Embassy told me that she learned, to her dismay, they have closed 80 of the 95 seminaries in that country. "When the Son of Man comes, will he find any faith on the earth?" (Luke 18:8)

The Lady who appeared in radiant whiteness to the Fatima children gave them a mission to suffer in reparation for sin and for the conversion of sinners, to save an unbelieving world where television projects a Godless society; where the words "denial", "penance" and "sacrifice" find no place in the news media; where worldly attachments hold us in their spell; where a cloak is thrown over sin.

When the angel sounds the trumpet to announce to the world that time shall be no more, what ineffable joy shall they experience who sacrificed what they were for what they were to become.

XII.
Diocesan Responses

Although there have been many dramatic incidents abroad during my years of travel with the statue, the majority of my time is spent in Diocesan Visitations in the United States.

The typical procedure is for a sponsoring group in a diocese to obtain their bishop's permission, and then contact the National Blue Army Center of the World Apostolate of Fatima, in Washington, New Jersey, to request a place on the schedule. The usual diocesan visit is about twenty-six days long. All the previous scheduling and arrangements are made by the local committee. Then, on the appointed day, the Statue and I will arrive for what is usually an inspiring, but also hectic, tour from place to place, preaching Our Lady's Fatima message.

It is this day to day effort that is the backbone of the Pilgrim Virgin visitation program. The extent of the local response varies, of course, from diocese to diocese. In some, Our Lady's message finds more receptive listeners than in others. But, the venerated image is and has been the vehicle for opening the way for grace to come into countless hearts and minds. Here are a few examples of the wonders of grace on an individual and collective basis.

A writer for the *Grand Rapids Press* wrote:

Maybe it's the lifelike eyes set in the cedarwood statue that makes people stop and stare and cry. Maybe it's the miraculous stories attributed to the International "Our Lady of Fatima" Statue which will be touring diocesan Roman Catholic Churches during the month of May. Maybe it's because Pope John Paul II publicly credited his surviving an assassin's bullets to Christ's Mother. . . . Whatever it is, whenever the statue is brought before believers, a look of awe crosses the viewer's face and the room becomes silent as people gather to pray.[1]

On June 22, 1984, the sun shone brightly, and so did God's grace through the statue which I took to Georgia Baptist Medical Center in Atlanta. A registered nurse, who is also a Baptist, wrote us:

Today I beheld for the first time an awesomely overwhelming sight: I saw the world famous statue of Our Lady of Fatima. I can't begin to tell you, indeed mere words are inadequate, how awe struck I was upon first viewing the Lady . . . my first impression could be humbly akin to the impression that the Blessed Virgin must have made upon Sister Lucia and the other two children of Fatima. . . .[2]

In the May/June issue of *Soul* magazine, Fr. Sylvester Scotti of Newberry, South Carolina, stated:

Our Lady came to us with almost a "silent message", touching individual people in acts of love and faith. Most people said they began to feel a quiet calm, a feeling of assurance that despite the evil around us we have special protection, a Mother of grand majesty reaching out to Her children. We seemed to feel that before a move of strength on Her part and the part of Her Son, She was asking for a reaching out of Love from her children.

Rev. Perry W. Dodds, St. Edward's Parish, Twin Falls, Idaho, in a letter to his parishioners dated February 23, 1983, stated:

> I believe that this Pilgrim Virgin Statue is something from Our Lady herself. . . . It will be a source of great comfort for us all to experience the enthusiasm always generated by the Pilgrim Virgin's visit. . . . [Her visit to] Twin Falls in 1979 created something of a spiritual explosion; many of you will remember what a singularly spiritual event it was . . . it will be a chance to renew and rekindle our devotion to Our Lady and pray most effectively for world peace.

Rev. Florian Fairbanks, O.S.B., St. Anthony Church, St. Anthony, North Dakota, said: "People who see this statue and hear the message can only become better Catholics."

Rev. Robert J. Fox, then of Redfield, South Dakota, in his "Theotokos", Vol. 9 #4, November 1983, wrote:

> Peace through Consecration to the Immaculate Heart of Mary was the theme as the International Pilgrim Virgin Statue travelled throughout the parishes, convents and care centers in the Sioux Falls Diocese. From the reports I have received, She has granted favors to many.

In St. Joseph's Church, Sioux City, Iowa, a young lady in a checkered blue and white dress was absorbed in thought as she stood before Our Lady's image. When I asked her opinion of the statue, she answered in one word: "Wow!"

One of the many churches in South Bend, Indiana that we visited had signs in the vestibule of the Church, made by second grade pupils, to welcome Our Lady. One sign that caught my imagination and eye was: "Welcome, Miss Heaven!"

Three airline stewardesses were admiring Our Lady's image in Sacred Heart Church, Tampa, Florida. One remarked that she had had the statue and myself as passengers on a flight. She smiled, and with a soft voice and a twinkle in her eyes, said: "I hosted her on United Airlines—I hope she hosts me in

Heaven because She is the Hostess of Heaven."

In April of 1985 I visited the Biloxi Diocese of Mississippi. Our Lady's statue received wonderful coverage from the newspapers and two television shows that we did on WLOX, Channel 13, "Good Morning South Mississippi." Sister Ignatius of Nativity B.V.M. school in Biloxi had her second graders write me letters of thank you. Here are a few of the letters:

> Thank you so much for bringing the beautiful statue to Biloxi, Mississippi. My class and I all watched you and Mary on television. You looked very good. I can not wait till it comes to Nativity. Oh, I am in Sister Ignatius's class.—Susan Mitchell

> I don't know how to thank you. Thank you for bringing the Pilgrim Virgin Statue to Biloxi. I can't wait till you and the statue come to our school. I pray for you and the statue every day and night. I love Mary and Jesus very much.—Mary Hankins

> Thank you for bringing the statue. I love you, Mr. Louie. How do you feel?—Virginia Cecil

> Mary, you're a winner!—Trae Mahoney

> We saw you on T.V. with Mother Mary; the statue is lovely. Will you buy me one?—Jeremy Cruthirds

> Mary, I love you. What is Heaven like?—Kristy Ellis

> I love Mary. I love Jesus and God too. Heaven must be nice. Do you have a scapular, Mary?—Raymond St. Amant

The fourth grade children of St. Joseph's Church, Cold Spring, Kentucky, were asked to write letters about Our Lady's visitation of November 4, 1981. Here are a few of the letters:

I felt like a whole new person. It was like my whole life was starting over. I felt that Mary was really there with us. I will never be that happy in my life. At that very moment I was full of joy and hope and love. I will start loving more than fighting. I will do what is right from now on.—Rhonda Saccone

When the statue came I felt like I was in Heaven. The statue was very nice. It gave me chills. It was the beautifull-est thing I ever saw in my life.—Kevan Brown

When Mary came to visit our church, my heart started beating faster as they carried her on the platform. I was very excited as the statue went past me. It was not only pretty, it was beautiful. I'm sure that everyone in the world would surely like to see it. And I am going to pray the Rosary every night and day because then there will be peace in the world if everyone would pray the rosary.—Angie Eschenback

I felt so wonderful before Mary Mother of God, as if she were really alive before me. Just to see her beauty fills my heart with joy and love. I will pray the Rosary every day with love and laughter. I felt overjoyed. You have changed my life by letting me live the Rosary. I love you Mary.—Jenny Neltner

One overcast, chilly day, in Duluth, Minnesota, a young mother carrying a baby and a freshly cut bouquet of flowers, neatly arranged, walked into the church and very politely asked, "Could I please place these flowers at the feet of Our Lady? I cut them from my garden." She continued,

I want Our Lady to have them in grateful appreciation for mending our marriage. Only Our Lord and Our Lady know the cold, dark years, full of many tears, I suffered. The inner turmoil was terrible. Now I have a deep, abiding joy. My husband has returned to the Sacraments; we pray the rosary every evening all because of Our Lady's visit four years ago when I challenged my husband to see Our Lady. He said something in him dormant came alive; he now wants to be a good father and loving husband.

Entering a nursing home in St. Louis, Missouri, the winds were gusty, the leaves rustling. A woman confined to a wheelchair, suffering from multiple sclerosis, was so bright, idealistic and enthusiastic that the nurses were amazed. She said that all of her life she wanted to go to Fatima to see the Lady but because of her illness, which struck her down early in life, she was not able to. "So the Lady came to see me!"

In St. Michael's Church, Biloxi, Mississippi, in April of 1985, I was fascinated by the lovely banner the Vietnamese made in honor of Our Lady's first visit in January 1980. The banner read:

QUEEN OF PEACE. Hail Queen of peace! We are Vietnamese; your people. We joyfully proclaim your holy name. We praise you, O Mary, full of grace. Your splendor shines upon us. You are our hope, and our peace.—Vietnamese Community in Biloxi

"Two men were behind bars. One looked out and saw mud, the other stars." One of the federal penitentiaries that we visited is in Atlanta, Georgia. The chaplain, beside himself with joy, remarked, "There is a real miracle" as he motioned for me to focus my attention on a dark-eyed, stocky inmate with an intense and almost haunted look as he stood before Our Lady's image, hands resting on her feet, eyes fixed on her eyes, rapt in thought. The surprised chaplain went on to say, "He is the hardest of the hard!" His fellow prisoners were in awe as they observed him, motionless, looking at her as an immigrant would look at the Statue of Liberty.

Other prisoners came, young and old, scarred and smooth, the Catholics and the curious. One young man, eyes begging, savored every moment. As he was about to leave, his pale-blue eyes moist, he asked for a rosary and a scapular.

A chorus of frogs welcomed the night outside of a church in St. Paul, Minnesota, after an evening service. A tall, slender man, middle-aged, was telling me of the graces he had received from the first visit of Our Lady's image three years previously. His heart pounded as he said, "I go to daily Mass and Holy Communion; pray a fifteen decade rosary daily; wear the Brown Scapular; make the Five First Saturdays—and I want to become a saint!" The man took a great delight in telling me that, "three years ago I didn't think this was possible."

"We not only converted to Catholicism since you were last here with the Virgin's statue, five years ago, but we have enthroned in our home the Sacred Heart of Jesus and the Immaculate Heart of Mary." These words flowed from a husband, holding his wife's hand, as he walked past me in the vestibule of St. Vibiana's Church, Los Angeles, California.

Father Louis Lohan of St. Lucy Church, Lucedale, Mississippi, was delighted to tell me that the son of Mrs. Betty H. Smith was most anxious to carry Our Lady's statue in procession in grateful appreciation for the cure he received over four years ago when the statue first visited the church. The boy, 11 years of age at the time, had a deteriorating hip for which there was no cure. The doctors informed the parents the boy would have to use crutches for life.

After many hours of prayer and veneration before the statue of Our Lady, the boy told his mother he had no more pain. Shortly thereafter, he refused to use his crutches. His mother insisted that he use them until the doctors could examine him. Upon examination, the doctors said that it was a miracle—that they had never seen a bone condition heal so perfectly.

On my fourteenth birthday, January 26, 1980 . . . I went to Keesler Air Force Base Chapel Two, to see her, after just finding out I had a chronic illness, cancer. I was greeted by Louis who escorted me to the Madonna where I touched her foot while he prayed with me. A feeling of deep warmth overcame me which words cannot express.

Now, after five years I have not only overcome cancer, but also a re-occurrence in November of 1984. Once again the Blessed Mother has given me the strength to get through hard, sickly and unpleasant times. I want to repay her by always loving her and telling people of the wondrous help she has given me.

The above statement was given to me on April 22, 1985, by Miss Patricia Nicovich Herrington in Biloxi, Mississippi.

At St. Louis Church, Sciota, New York, the priest remarked that there certainly was something miraculous about this statue: "It was the first time that everyone rushed to the front pews leaving the back pews vacant—a miracle!"

In 1981, in Bayou Blue, Louisiana, at St. Louis Church, red roses welcomed the Queen of the Rosary—one red rose for every year of Christianity. It was the most roses the famed image has received since I have been the escort. It was a magnificent sight beyond description. In that church Our Lady touched three hearts. A family, mother, father and son, received the grace to come back to the sacraments after having been away for 12 years.

The Carmelite Sisters of Lake Elmo, Minnesota were beside themselves with great joy when Our Lady's statue graced their dwelling for an all-night vigil. In the early morning the shrill ringing of the door bell, a discordant noise invading the silence and solitude of the cloister, was the indication the statue was to depart shortly. "Bring her back soon, please," said one of the sisters with a smile touching her face. "That would be difficult due to the schedule. She is booked almost two years in advance." You could hear the buzzing of tense, excited voices as sister came back with, "Certainly you have a few days off during the year—and don't you have a vacation?" "Yes, but it wouldn't be practical to come for one day, and the mileage is prohibitive." The sisters were determined. Suddenly a map of the United States was presented to me. "Look at the map and tell us just how far Flint, Michigan is from Lake Elmo, Minnesota," said Sister Teresa with a somewhat sheepish look on her cheerful, cherub face. Before I could answer, Sister Rose quickly interjected, "It is only a few inches, and 'inch by inch it's a cinch; yard by yard it's hard.'" We all had a hearty laugh as all of the sisters gave a little whoop of delight in their mirth. The following year, during vacation time, the 765 mile drive was a breeze.

The bulletin of St. Boniface Church, Walhalla, N.D., July 21, 1985, stated:

> We have the honor of a special guest coming to our parish July 25. "What an honor this is, that the Mother of my Lord should visit me." (Luke 1:43) Let each one in our parish make a great effort to make this a special day in our lives. When we know someone is coming to visit, we plan and prepare to spend as much time as possible with them. The Pilgrim Virgin Statue of Mary is a special guest.

The World-Herald of Omaha, Nebraska, Oct. 6, 1985, carried an article on the statue's visitation which quoted Auxiliary Bishop Anthony Milone saying, "The statue's beauty is enough to melt the heart of a very hard person." Within one week I was in Our Lady of Lourdes rectory talking with two priests. One of the priests told me that a man out of the church for fourteen years came to confession to him stating that he had committed every sin in the book—"but that Lady brought me back!"

The bulletin of St. John the Evangelist Church, Valley, Nebraska, dated Oct. 13, 1985, stated:

> WELCOME! Mother of God, as you bless our Parish Family of St. John with your presence as "The Pilgrim Virgin of Fatima". Where you are, there your Son, Jesus, is! Open our hearts to the message you give us through the children of Fatima. May your visitation bring to each of us . . . to our Parish Family as a whole . . . a deeper realization of the supernatural dimensions of our being: love for Him in the love and service we give to one another . . . a deep reverence and affirmation of the brothers and sisters created in His image and likeness, redeemed by His life and passion, and death and resurrection.

In November of 1985 Our Lady's statue was in Lowell, Massachusetts, at St. Joseph's Shrine, where 7,000 people venerated her and 3,000 went to the Sacrament of Penance—the most confessions I have ever witnessed. Fifteen priests were kept busy for three days hearing the confessions. Earlier at this same church, a Mrs. Jeanne Connelly confided to me that she was cured of bronchitis when she touched the statue in June of 1976, my first visitation to the Boston area.

In March of 1982, in Dallas, Texas, the pastor of a church in that diocese confided to me, with tears in both eyes, that he found that his devotion to Our Lady was rejuvenated merely from observing the statue being carried in procession down the center aisle while he stood in the sanctuary.

In the Green Bay Diocese of Wisconsin, May of 1984, a young man, twenty two years of age told me that he received a powerful grace from Our Lady concerning his vocation. He now knew for certain that Our Lord wanted him to become a priest.

The Carmelite Sisters of the Divine Heart of Jesus, Kirkwook, Missouri, wrote in their Vol. 11, No. 1, October 1982, newsletter:

> . . . Our Lady's beautiful image was enshrined fittingly beside her Son, exposed for adoration in the Blessed Sacrament. . . . You cannot help but feel Our Lady's real, moral presence as you kneel before her image. Her most pure love seems to radiate gently and continuously from her sweet, soft countenance, and her eyes, though obviously aglow with the fire of divine love, are calm and serene, and perhaps not a little sad, for she knows better and feels more acutely the great and urgent need for reparation to her Immaculate Heart. The longing in her eyes seems to mirror and enkindle the secret longing in your own heart for her divine Son. She is an enigma—at once a beautiful woman on fire with the love of her God—vital and dynamic—and the sweetest, gentlest, and purest of mothers.

On the Island of Hawaii we were warmly welcomed by a huge crowd which included Mayor Herbert T. Matayoshi and other dignitaries. Mayor Matayoshi presented me with a document in honor of Our Lady which read:

COUNTY OF HAWAII
OFFICE OF THE MAYOR

WHEREAS, The original International Pilgrim Virgin statues were blessed at Fatima in 1947; and

WHEREAS, for thirty years the two International statues have travelled throughout the world to create peace in the world; and

WHEREAS, the statues have become a binding force to unite the people of different nations around the world; and

WHEREAS, the statues have been instrumental in our quest for world peace and security.

NOW, THEREFORE, I HERBERT T. MATAYOSHI, Mayor of the County of Hawaii, do hereby proclaim December 29, 1977, and December 30, 1977, as THE INTERNATIONAL PILGRIM VIRGIN DAYS.

Upon the above being read, people stepped forward and placed multi-colored leis on Our Lady's statue. So many were placed on the image, that all one could see of the four-foot statue was her head.

Visiting the Hawaiian Islands was a memorable experience that shall be cherished. The flight to the island of Molokai filled us with anticipation. Upon landing, we travelled by car some twelve miles to Kalaupapa—the sacred ground where Fr. Damian and Joseph Dutton led lives of heroic dedication as they ministered to the needs of the lepers. After visiting the graves of these two holy men, we went to the leprosarium; an inconceivable joy filled the wards of the hospital as we took Our Lady's image from ward to ward. One felt close to God in the presence of these victim souls. The leprosy was taking its toll by disfiguring them pitifully; but a loving God used this disease as a tool to beautify their souls, and save sinners. They radiated peace, joy and resignation. The leprosy wasn't contagious; their spirit was.

Of all the islands of Hawaii, Lanai had the most ecumenical spirit. We were welcomed at the airport on the small island by over 105 cars—I believe every car on the island was present. A motorcade wound its way into the town of Lanai City to the accompaniment of a band, predominantly Protestant, playing one Marian hymn after another as we found our way to the Catholic Church. So many leis were placed upon Our Lady's statue that she was buried with the flowers. A good portion had to be removed and placed at her feet. Hawaii was a reaffirmation of what we found all over the world: people were hungry for devotion to the Mother of God.

Often a question posed to me was, "Which is the greatest diocese you have ever visited?" No hesitation on my part: the Scranton Diocese of Pennsylvania! The spiritual director is a great credit to the Church; Christ-like and Marian-minded, his life is wrapped-up in Jesus and Mary. He welcomed Our Lady's image and myself at the Scranton-Wilkes-Barre (Avoca) airport on May 1, 1976, with an estimated 5,000 people, in a downpour of rain which failed to dampen the spirit of the huge crowd. Fr. Anthony Noviello had worked tirelessly for sixteen months in preparation for the gala event. Here are his words about the month's visitation:

> Never before such enthusiasm, such outbursts of joy at the arrival of Our Lady! Never before such fervid tears and prayers for moral or even a physical miracle! The people who numbered in the hundreds upon hundreds would increase to thousands upon thousands as she moved from church to church throughout the diocese of Scranton to greet her children and to exhort them to more prayer, more sacrifice, more penance! Our Lady was set to cut a swath in the diocesan hills and dales, towns and villages, cities and suburbs, in a trek which would level and make smooth all that

lay before her, eventually marking one of her greatest
triumphs in the hearts of people who needed her most. . . . [3]

Mayor Walter Lisman, in the presence of nine area clergy-
men, proclaimed the month of May as "FATIMA MONTH,"
issuing an edict to that effect. Thirty thousand people a day
poured into the various churches to glimpse the Lady and catch
the message. 750,000 paid homage to her before the month was
over. Some cities saw lines four abreast, one quarter of a mile
long. Never have I seen such an outpouring of faith. Fr.
Noviello described our departure at the airport:

> Tears abounded. The atmosphere was tense. It couldn't
> happen; it must not happen. The cries, the sighs, the tears,
> the sobs could not restrain her, other children were an-
> xiously awaiting her. . . .
> Just moments from being removed from the float on which
> she had ridden, the man who made it . . . handed the statue
> to its custodian who seized her firmly and in an unexpected
> move thrust the statue into the sky and shouted: "Up until
> now, she has been yours. Now she's all mine!" The shouts
> and cheers were deafening, for Our Lady seemed to have
> dropped right out of the sky with the sun to her back. What a
> thrilling sight; cameras clicked amid shouts of joy. Our sad-
> ness was quickly turned to joy. The tears that fell now served
> only to express our happiness. . . . Each returned to his or
> her home now not with sadness but with inexplicable joy in
> their hearts.
> But in one sense the drama never ended for Mary's mes-
> sage, like the seed that fell into good ground, produced fruit
> a hundredfold. [4]

And Fr. Noviello cites the evidence: recitation of the Rosary, May crownings, scapular enrollment, holy hours, first
Saturday devotions, Rosary rallies, Diocesan family Rosary,
consecration to Mary's Immaculate Heart.

The visits of Our Lady invariably produce some good
result. It might be an official proclamation—as when the gov-

ernor of Utah declared October of 1984 to be "Prayers for Peace
Month" partly because of our International Rosary March. Or it
might be a purely personal response—as when a listener
phoned radio station WNEB in Worcester, Massachusetts to
say that our recently-broadcast Fatima message "should be
preached from all the pulpits of the world!" One of my favorite
incidents, however, came on one of numerous visits Our
Lady's statue made to the twenty-four cloistered Carmelites in
Long Beach, California. After one talk to these lovely sisters, I
was answering questions. One sister, very petite and pious,
said: "I don't want to ask a question, I just want to make a
statement: you lead a rather austere life, don't you?" I chuckled
in reply, "Yes and I believe it is more austere than you Carmelites live. I would like to prove it to you."

"I have been in your diocese for almost a month and have
averaged four and one half hours of sleep per night due to the
heavy schedule [72 churches in 26 days]. I know you sisters get
at least seven hours of sleep per night. You have a bed to sleep
in; I never know where I will sleep. And you have the same bed
every night; I have to adjust to a different one every night. You
have a bedroom all to yourself; I don't have that luxury—
sometimes I end up sleeping in a hospital, church, school, jail,
department store, and three times I have found myself sleeping next to coffins!"

"You have a desk to write letters; I usually have to write on
my knee. You get three meals a day, even if frugal; I never
know where the next meal is coming from [many times I have
had to cram my pockets with jelly beans for instant energy to
give a talk in case of emergency]. You have a place to wash your
clothes; I have to search for a source. You have eight hours a
day for prayers, meditation, contemplation. If I get one-half
hour a day to myself, it is a bonus."

"You have twenty-four nuns to encourage and inspire each
other; I am all alone. Everyone loves a cloistered Carmelite
nun; I am an enemy until I can feel the vibes of those about to

receive Our Lady's image and myself. You can be relaxed as your life is somewhat routine; I always have to prove myself daily to those about to hear the message. You know where a restroom is; I never do. In this job you have no roots; you are as much a pilgrim as the statue is."

Ironically enough, shortly after rattling off this litany of my comparisons to the Carmelite nuns, Mrs. Audrey Stoken, the coordinator of Charleston, South Carolina, whom I had worked with for the visitation in her diocese, sent me a picture of Our Lady with a quotation from Matthew printed on the back (with modifications):

SACRIFICE TO FOLLOW MARY
Matthew 9:19-20

Then a scribe came and said to Him, "Master, I will follow Thee wherever Thou goest." But Jesus [Mary] said to him, "the foxes have dens, and the birds of the air have nests; but the Son of Man has nowhere to lay His head."

NOTES

[1]Theresa D. McClellan, *The Grand Rapids Press*, Saturday, May 8, 1982, Grand Rapids, Michigan.
[2]Hardy, Shirley, RN, Letter addressed to Blue Army, 1555 Adelaide St., S.E., Warren, Ohio.
[3]Personal report from Fr. Noviello to author, dated December 12, 1981.
[4]*Ibid.*

XIII.
Last Appeal

Pilgrimages to the Philippines and Central America in 1985 have shown once again the great importance of the Pilgrim Virgin and her message. On December 4th, 1985, at 7:00 a.m., our Philippine Airline 747 Jumbo-Jet, flight PR 107, began its initial approach for a landing in Manila, some 90 miles away, to be warmly welcomed by a lovely rainbow on the right side of the plane, and Captain Ortiz's soft and pleasant voice:

Ladies and gentlemen, on behalf of Philippine Airlines, I would like to welcome Our Blessed Mother of Christ, Our Lady of Fatima, who is one of our passengers, to the Philippines. She is on a world tour on a mission of peace, good will and happiness. We are indeed fortunate and deeply honored by this rare and highly important visit of our beloved lady to our country. We are sure she will receive a very warm welcome in Manila. God bless us all. Thank you.

Only after having landed at the huge airport in Manila with my precious charge would I learn that Jaime Cardinal L. Sin, Archbishop of Manila, had made a special effort to rally his people through a widely distributed brochure:

It is indeed of great significance that the International Pilgrim Virgin of Fatima comes to our country. . .as we go through our nation's darkest hour.

Let us open wide the doors of our hearts, then, to Mary, and give Her a warm welcome, as She comes to our land. For in opening our hearts to her, we thereby open our hearts to Her Son, Our Divine Redeemer.

Let us heed her message of prayer and penance, and make of ourselves Her indefatigable apostles of peace, that Her promise of Russia's conversion and world peace may at last dawn upon our war-torn earth.

Such sincere and firm resolve on our part is the best gift our hearts can give to our Heavenly Mother, as She comes to visit our beloved land, that if we faithfully keep it, our country and our people shall soon rise from the present morass we are in, just as Her Divine Son, Jesus, rose triumphantly from the dead on that first Easter morn.

Other dignitaries followed suit. Their comments are quoted here to show their intense concern for Our Lady's message and need for Our Lady's help. Archbishop of Lingayen-Dagupan, Federico G. Limon, S.V.D., D.D., declared:

I venture to say that "Our Blessed Mother goes around the world sounding her last appeal for reconciliation. We fear that this call is not listened to by many." Mary should teach us through her message at Fatima the conversion of hearts, a condition for peace with God.

The Mayor of Manila, Ramon D. Bagatsing, likewise strongly supported Our Lady's visit:

It is heartening to comprehend that Our Lady of Fatima shall arrive at a time when we, as a Christian people, embark on meaningful activities for national reconciliation. May Her message ring loud and clear that humanity should go back to piety and reverence to achieve world peace founded on love, trust and cooperation.

Finally, the Apostolic Nuncio to the Philippines, Bruno Torigliani, iced the cake:

> This is a timely occasion for us to recall the intention of the Holy Father, Pope John Paul II, who, three years ago in Fatima, had consecrated the whole world to the Immaculate Heart of Mary and who had asked the Bishops of the world to do the same. In the act of entrusting to Our Lady, the Pope said, "Mother of the Church! enlighten the people of God along the paths of faith, hope and love! Help us to live in the truth to the consecration of Christ for the entire human family of the modern world." As we welcome the image of Our Lady of Fatima, let us join with the Holy Father in his prayer to "help us conquer the menace of evil, which so easily takes root in the hearts of the people," so that we could show the infinite power of the redemption of Jesus Christ.

I read, over and over, Jaime Cardinal Sin's words, "It is indeed of great significance that the International Pilgrim Virgin of Fatima comes to our country . . . as we go through our nation's darkest hour." Clearly, his great dread was that his country might be taken over by atheistic communism, for he himself had told his people just six months previously,

> If we fail in this vision of conversion and Christian transformation of our society, then communism with its promise of economic equality will overtake us and overrun this nation. They promise economic equality but without God, without love. Communism establishes community with the barrel of a gun.
> In a distorted way, communism endeavors to do what we, the Church, are failing to do. Were we truly Christian, communism would not even be a dream.[1]

Just as Cardinal Sin had warned his people about the perils of communism, Pope Pius XI, in his Encyclical Letter *Divini Redemptoris* had warned the entire world,

> . . . seeing that the whole world is anxious for peace, the
> leaders of communism now pose as the most ardent support-
> ers of every movement for the establishment of international
> concord; at the same time, however, they continue to foment
> in each nation a class warfare which causes rivers of blood to
> flow, and at home pile up huge armaments on the plea of
> safeguarding internal security.[2]

Like a spider-cancer, atheistic communism has spread its
deadly tentacles around the world, engulfing country after
country, spilling the blood of millions. Since the Soviet Communist State was created on November 8, 1917, following the
Bolshevik revolution, the following countries and lands have
been swallowed up by the atheistic communists:

Ukraine	Estonia	North Korea	Mozambique
Aszerbaijan	Bulgaria	Sakhalin Island	Ethiopia
Kazakhstan	Poland	China	South Yemen
Armenia	Romania	Tibet	Afghanistan
Belorussia	Tana-Tuva	Cuba	Nicaragua
Georgia	Hungary	South Vietnam	Suriname
Mongolia	Yugoslavia	North Vietnam	Kurile Islands
Russia	Albania	Laos	Saint Tromain
Latvia	East Germany	Cambodia	Guyana
Lithuania	Czechoslovakia	Angola	Chad

Italy is ripe to be toppled into the communist bloc. Two of
India's largest states are communist. Central America is
threatened. Spain has shown leanings to the left. Mexico is not
stable and is currently on a teeter-totter. Brazil, Peru, and
Chile are in turmoil.

While he was the pastor of Our Lady of Fatima Church in
Ludlow, Massachusetts, I spent some time with Fr. Manuel
Rocha, the interpreter selected for Mr. William Thomas
Walsh, who wrote perhaps the most popular book on Fatima.
Fr. Rocha told me that one of the questions Mr. Walsh asked
him to translate to Sister Lucia during a three hour interview

on the afternoon of July 15, 1946, while she was still Sister Maria das Dores, a Dorothean Sister at Vilar, near Porto, Portugal was "In your opinion, will every country, without exception, be overcome by communism?" Her pale brown eyes staring into his, a "little dimple on each cheek", she answered "yes." Fr. Rocha related to me that Mr. Walsh wanted to be positive about the answer and therefore repeated the question adding "and does that mean the United States of America too?" Sister Lucia answered "yes."

Sister Lucia went on to say:

> What Our Lady wants is that the Pope and all the bishops in the world consecrate Russia to her Immaculate Heart on one special day. If this is done, she will convert Russia and there will be peace. If it is not done, the errors of Russia will spread through every country in the world.[3]

Fr. Rocha, as well as Mr. Walsh,[4] felt that the consecration had not been made because Our Lady's wishes had not yet been carried out. People must say the Rosary, perform sacrifices, make the five first Saturdays, and wear the Brown Scapular as a sign of consecration to Her Immaculate Heart.

Archbishop Fulton J. Sheen, one of the world's greatest experts on communism, said,

> The two great forces of the Mystical Body of Christ and the Mystical Body of the Antichrist are beginning to draw up their battle lines for the catastrophic combat. Communism is the Mystical Body of the Antichrist, its invisible head is the devil, its members are not merely those who deny God, but those who challenge God, its Peter and Paul are Marx and Lenin, its Bible is Das Kapital; and its temporal city is the Kremlin.
>
> We are living the days of the Apocalypse—the last days of our era.[5]

Surely it was with these things in mind that Cardinal Sin crowned Our Lady in the airport. With deep humility and the greatest reverence he kissed the foot of the image. He personally carried the famous statue to the flat-bed truck decked out proudly with scores of native greens and flowers awaiting its unique cargo.

We climbed onto the truck and held Our Lady's image firmly on the pedestal made to accommodate her. The engine ignited. The clutch engaged. The gears shifted. We were in motion.

Dressed neatly in immaculate white shirts and navy trousers, twelve motorcycle policemen led our caravan. They drove 750 c.c. Hondas and 600 c.c. B.M.W.s as they wended their way ahead of us. Sirens wailed. Excitement was high. Following closely behind were six police cars filled with high ranking officers. The caravan strung out over a mile as we made a right hand turn unto Roxas Boulevard on our way to the cathedral, Our Lady of Perpetual Help.

Overhead was an impressive sight—the helicopters accompanying us. One dropped tens of thousands of rose petals on Our Lady's image and the caravan. The other dropped 50,000 leaflets, 3 1/2" x 5", showing a picture of the statue with the following message beneath, "Bring your family and join two million people praying the rosary on the occasion of the visit of the International Pilgrim image of Our Lady of Fatima. Let's pray for our family, for our country, for peace, on Dec. 8th, Sunday, 3:30 P.M., at Luneta Park."

Traffic going both ways was jammed for miles. Horns beeped without let-up! People lining both sides of the boulevard waved white handkerchiefs, shouting joyfully "Mother Mary we love you" or "Welcome Mother Mary."

Ten thousand people were inside of the cathedral with another 6,000 outside. On the huge pillars of the cathedral were gigantic banners 25 feet high and 3 feet wide saying "Ave Maria" in blue and white. In the sanctuary to the left was an enormous sign "Mama Mary we love you." An incredible welcome: an all night vigil was in store.

After a welcome sleep in the Manila Hotel, we were back at the airport taking Our Lady to Davao City with Cardinal Sin and a committee of 18 people consisting of newspaper reporters, photographers, committee members and myself.

Davao is the third largest city in the Philippines and boasts almost 1,000,000 people. At St. Peter's Cathedral Mayor Elias B. Lopez gave us a most cordial, heartwarming welcome. This was the same church that Pope John Paul II visited in February of 1981. On Easter Sunday of that year a bomb would be exploded in the same church at the 7:00 P.M. mass killing eight people and injuring dozens. Archbishop Antonio Li Mabutas, D.D. would warmly greet each and every one of us over a sumptuous meal that he made available for us after the services attended by thousands.

At 11:00 a.m. we boarded the plane for our departure to Cebu, the second largest city in the Philippines with slightly over 1,000,000 people. I have never experienced a welcome like Our Lady received from the moment we touched down at Mactan Airport to the moment we left! It was unprecedented, awesome! I was told that because of the visit of Our Lady's image, a national holiday had been proclaimed with everyone being released from work to welcome Our Lady. Mactan Airport was the spot where Ferdinand Magellan had landed in the year 1521, planting the first Christian cross into the soil. It would be from that very point that we would start our motorcade, passing through one million people lining both sides of the street as we traveled fifteen miles through the cities of Lapulapu, Mandaue and on into Cebu!

Jubilant school children, by the tens of thousands, were waving blue and white paper flags, mounted on little sticks, to their Heavenly Mother's image, being held on the truck by Fr. Lorenzo Guerrero, S.J., Howard Dee and myself, under a shower of flowers all the way.

The tremendous joy and excitement generated by the immense crowd lifted moods. For fifteen miles over one million people joyfully and lovingly threw flowers at Our Lady's statue, cheering ardently as the image passed. Spirits were sky-high. Children jumped up and down with glee. At the designated stopping place for praying the decades of the Rosary, a minimum of 50,000 people were present, praying with a communicable fervor. Cameras flicked constantly.

December 7th found us in Iloilo City where over one hundred thousand would manifest their love to Our Lady. In the morning, very early, I had breakfast with Cardinal Sin. Bacon and eggs, coffee and toast. Though always jovial, he became serious as he asked me, "Louie, why does the statue cry?" "Because of sin, your excellency." My face flushed warm and red after I realized that his name is Sin. I quickly injected: "Because people break the 10 commandments . . . some refer to them as 10 suggestions." I continued, "We have hardened our hearts so that, I feel, God works in unusual ways to bring us back to our senses, like allowing statues to weep." And Pope John Paul II said "If the statue of Our Lady weeps, it is because she has reason to weep."

In all of my travels and experiences with the sacred image, nothing can compare to what happened in Manila on December 8th. The city dressed with over 1,000 posters on buildings and bill-boards with life-sized pictures of Our Lady saying, "I'm here. Let's pray." Over 500 banners in blue and white 20 feet high, 2 feet wide, hanging from the tops of telephone poles greeted everyone with "People at Prayer" and "People at Peace."

At 3:30 P.M. two million people stood with umbrellas braving a blistering sun at Luneta Park to pray the Rosary for world peace, to attend Mass concelebrated by 126 priests, 5 bishops, and Cardinal Sin, and to hear the message of Fatima.

The correspondent of the Malaya newspaper, Mr. Noli Alparce, in his article the following day said, "An estimated 1,500,000 Filipino faithful devotées joined the family rosary rally yesterday at the Rizal [Luneta] Park.[6] Mr. Alparce did admit, later, that he kept the figure low. Others said it was the largest crowd they had ever seen. The chief of police requested 1,600 officers for the event. He personally told me that he had never seen the likes of such a huge crowd and that it was in excess of two million.

The programme for the historic afternoon would begin with the recitation of Our Lady's favorite prayer, the Rosary. What a sight, what a sound—two million voices rapping on the doors of Heaven supplicating the Queen of Heaven and the Queen of Peace to intercede with Her Son, the Prince of Peace, begging peace for the world. Surely Our Lady would win. Surely God would not refuse Her!

St. Gemma Galgani, a 20th century stigmatist, one day was interceding with Our Lord for the soul of a certain sinner in Italy. As Gemma pleaded for mercy, Our Lord recounted one by one his frightful and abnormal sins. After Our Lord had refused three times, St. Gemma Galgani said to Him: "Then I shall ask your Mother." Our Lord answered: "In that case, I cannot refuse you." An hour later the great sinner in question came to the confessor of the saint and made his full confession.

Since "Prayer is man's strength and God's weakness", and Our Lord can refuse Our Lady nothing, we can be sure that Our Lady won us ample time to reform our lives, to continue pleading through the Rosary for peace and to continue living the message of Fatima with great hope that Russia will be converted and we will have an era of Peace.

The Rosary over, it was only fitting that the famed "Rosary Priest", Fr. Patrick Peyton, deliver a talk on the power and importance of the Rosary. This was followed immediately by the Holy Sacrifice of the Mass with Cardinal Sin delivering a compelling homily, "Renewal of Morality." After the Mass, Cardinal Sin introduced me, and I spoke on the message of Fatima. The First Lady of the land, Imelda Marcos, handed the crown of the Pilgrim Virgin to Msgr. Josefino Ramirez, who would crown the statue for Cardinal Sin.

The phenomenal services completed, the people lingered

tranquilly for hours until midnight. They were directed in two
enormous lines past Our Lady's image, many paying their
farewell salute. Some flashed pictures. Some simply stood in
awe or admiration. Some prayed. Some cried. Some fought
back tears.

At midnight, with great difficulty, we removed the statue
and placed her in the cathedral for a final all-night vigil
attended by record crowds. Early in the morning we made
three quick visits to convents, trying to make Our Lady's image
available to as many as we possibly could before her departure
from their soil at 5:00 p. m. Sisters of Mercy, Pink Sisters and
Carmelites would all welcome their Lady with hearts on fire
with love for Her. Each convent could only enjoy her presence
for a maximum of fifteen minutes. Every minute was filled with
prayer, song, love.

Our Lady's visitation to the Philippines was a colossal and
profound success, and I had to leave with Her image for
another troubled spot of the world, Central America. We were
to arrive in Belize (formerly British Honduras) on December
14 with hopes of getting into Guatemala and Mexico.

On the front page of the *Reporter*, the largest paper in
Belize, this caption was carried along with a lovely picture of
the statue: "Fatima Pilgrim Statue on Visit to Belize." The
article read,

> During the month of October Belize was host to the
> British Sovereign, Queen Elizabeth II, who paid her first
> visit to these shores. For three days during the month of
> December another queen, Mary spouse of Joseph of the
> Royal House of David and Queen of all the Americas and the
> World, will be sending an image of Herself, the Inter-
> national Pilgrim Statue of Our Lady of Fatima, to Belize.[7]

Three weeks later the same paper would carry a different photo
along with this caption: "Pilgrim Statue Warms Belize Roman
Catholics." It continued:

The four foot statue, carved with intricate care from Brazilian Cedar wood, is perhaps the most famous statue in the world, widely regarded as a miraculous statue through which Mary, the Lady of Fatima, recruits hundreds of thousands of Christians each year to live nobler, more saintly lives.

From the moment the statue arrived on Belize soil aboard the Tan-Sahsa aircraft and removed from its protective padded covering until the moment it left on pilgrim tour along the Northern Road, the statue was continuously surrounded by pious and admiring people who showered it with roses and flowers and surrounded it with lighted candles.

At Holy Redeemer Cathedral, the church remained full throughout a prayer vigil which went way past midnight and when the statue was taken to St. Catherine Academy and Pallotti Convent for a brief visit, the students lingered on, not wanting to see it taken away.[8]

The Catholic Diocesan paper told about the coming of the statue:

In the light of the atomic and hydrogen bombs, Star Wars, the expansion of communism, secularism and materialism of the 20th century, God sent Mary to Fatima in Portugal in 1917 . . . to save the whole world from military disaster and from Hell itself!

The message of Mary to the three little children at Fatima is simple but grave: Pray the Rosary daily. Abstain from sin yourself, and do penance for the sins of others. If not, a Third World War far more devastating than any previous, will destroy many nations.[9]

Belize is a very small country with 155,000 people. From the Ordinary, his excellency Bishop Osmond Martin, and the laity I received the warmest, most loving reception. Everyone showed their admiration and affection for Our Lady with sparkling eyes when they came to venerate the statue at the Cathedral. Bishop Martin gave a timely and excellent homily:

. . . There is a spiritual combat going on between the forces of good and the forces of evil. This combat goes on within the individual, within society and within the universe. One force represents the reign of goodness, the other represents the reign of evil. One represents life, the other death. The reality is that you and I are not mere spectators of this combat; rather, willingly and unwillingly, we have become an integral part of the enfleshed good or evil. For if you are not gathering, then you are scattering; if you are neither cold nor hot, then you are lukewarm.

He continued on:

. . . There is a type of unhappy situation today within the Christian community. There are religious groups that are determined to demolish the Catholic faith, its traditions and its religious practices. . . . The words Blessed Virgin Mary trip off a volcanic eruption of anger in the minds and hearts of religious fundamentalists. The honour paid to Mary by Catholics is looked upon as diabolic. Her statues and images have been smashed to pieces by Catholics who are now converts to fundamental beliefs and are as hateful and angry as their mentors. Do you call this behavior Christian? When we honor Mary in whatever form, we honor her in the shadow of the greatest honor bestowed on her by God—to be the Mother of our Savior. When we respect her, we respect her in the shadow of the great respect shown her by her Son—our Savior. When we take her to be our heavenly Mother, we take her as a gentle Mother given to us by her dying Son—our Savior. If you are a genuine Christian, never be ashamed of your natural mother or your heavenly mother because maternity is God's gift to humanity. If you are a true Christian, never be ashamed of honoring Mary, because God first honored her.

Belize is the smallest country I have taken Our Lady's image to. But they had probably the heaviest schedule of any foreign country I have visited. They took advantage of every possible minute that the famed image would grace their soil.

After the Mass was completed in the Cathedral at about 8:10 p.m., the programme continued with:

8:15 P.M. - Recitation of Rosary
8:30 P.M. - First Talk by Mr. Kaczmarek
9:00 P.M. - Recitation of Rosary
9:15 P.M. - Second Talk by Mr. Kaczmarek
9:45 P.M. - Recitation of Rosary
10:00 P.M - Silent Meditation
10:15 P.M - Scripture Reading by Mr. John Riedell
11:00 P.M - Song
11:05 P.M - Third Talk by Mr. Kaczmarek
11:30 P.M - Song
11:35 P.M. - Fourth Talk by Mr. Kaczmarek
12:00 Midnight - Closing Hymn

It was 1:30 a.m. before I got to bed. I tossed and turned before I settled into slumber. The last thing I recalled is that I had seen a rainbow on the left side of the plane just before we landed in Belize, while I had seen a rainbow on the right side of the plane before we landed in Manila. I tried to figure out the significance of each but was sound asleep before I could.

They had me up at 4:00 a.m. I had had but two-and-a-half hours of sleep! Staring me in the face was the program for the day:

5:00 A.M. - Guadalupe serenade enroute to Cathedral
5:30 A.M. - Mass in honor of Our Lady
6:30 A.M. - Breakfast
8:00 A.M. - Visit and Talk at St. Catherine Academy
9:00 A.M. - T.V., Radio, and Press Interview
12:45 P.M. - Depart for "Our Lady of the Way" Church, Ladyville
1:00 P.M. - Talk, Rosary, song at Our Lady of the Way Church

3:00 P.M. - Leave for Orange Walk

At Orange Walk I was handed a program similar to the above. From jet-lag coupled with these hectic programmes, my body was begging sleep. Everyone was apologizing for the heavy schedule but always with a smile. I was always jokingly, saying, "You're not sorry, you're smiling!"

People in Chetumal, Mexico, begged us to bring Our Lady to them. We obliged by granting them four hours. They made all the necessary arrangements and welcomed us as we crossed the border with a huge gathering of people carrying the freshest flowers of their land for Our Lady. We had a caravan, led by a police officer, to Our Lady of Guadalupe Church. People all along the route showed the greatest reverence and respect for the Lady of Fatima as she visited their fine city.

The people of the Third World are painfully conscious of the evils of atheistic communist regimes, and of the sins of men. Their magnificent reception of Our Lady testifies to their great concern for the future of their families, their nations and the entire world.

What will that future be? One of the last questions Mr. William Thomas Walsh asked Lucia in his long interview was, "Have you had any revelation from Our Lady about the end of the world?" She could not answer that question; can we?

Our Lady spoke of the annihilation of nations at Fatima if we did not heed her requests. Ironically, we now have weapons that can destroy the world, and man has never made a weapon that he has never used. Three personal coincidences recently impressed this problem on my mind once again.

First, while I was escorting Our Lady's statue in Oak Ridge, Tennessee, my dear mother was called into eternity with God. Oak Ridge is where the atom bomb was created under the code name "Manhattan Project". Secondly, my mother passed away on August 3, 1982 and was laid to rest on August 6—the day that the atom bomb was dropped on Hiroshima. Third, recently I visited Chanute Air Force Base in Rantoul, Illinois where I was stationed in the U.S. Air Force for several years. Directly in the front of the barracks I occupied, to my astonishment, is the famous "Enola Gay" B-29 Heavy Bomber that dropped the first atom bomb.

Three days after I returned to the United States with Our Lady's image from our Latin America Pilgrimage, I received a Christmas card from Bishop Osmond Martin. He wrote, "Louis, my people and I were very appreciative of your visit. You, the statue of Our Lady and your message came at a time that we really needed you." And so it goes the world over. Everyone needs Our Lady.

That we may have a world in peace—not pieces—please, God, give us the grace to change our lives while there is still time, and to fully respond to Our Lady's requests at Fatima so that we may witness the reign of grace, the conversion of Russia, and the coming of true peace—the wonders she performs.

NOTES

[1]Sin, Jaime Cardinal, D.D., *Banquet for Mary*, St. Paul Publications, Pasay, Metro Manila, 3129, p. 12.

[2]Pius XI, Pope, *Divini Redemptoris*, Catholic Truth Society, 38 to 40 Eccleston Square, London, W.W.1, p. 43.

[3]Walsh, William Thomas, *Our Lady of Fatima*, Image Books, Garden City, New York, p. 221.

[4]*Ibid.*

[5]Sheen, Bishop Fulton J., Ph.D., D.D., *The World's First Love*, Image Books, Garden City, New York, p. 202.

[6]Alparce, Mr. Noli, *Malaya*, Manila, Philippines, Dec. 9, 1985, Monday, Vol. IV, No. 327, p. 1.

[7]*The Reporter*, Belize City, Belize, Central America, Vol. 18, No. 43, Sunday, Nov. 24, 1985, p. 1.

[8]*Ibid.*, Number 43, Sunday, Dec. 15, 1985, p. 1.

[9]Pollard, Nick, Sr., *The Christian Herald*, Belize City, Belize, Central America, Vol. 6, No. 4, Dec. 1985, p. 1.

Photographs

The first Pilgrim Virgin statue.

The second (current) Pilgrim Virgin statue.

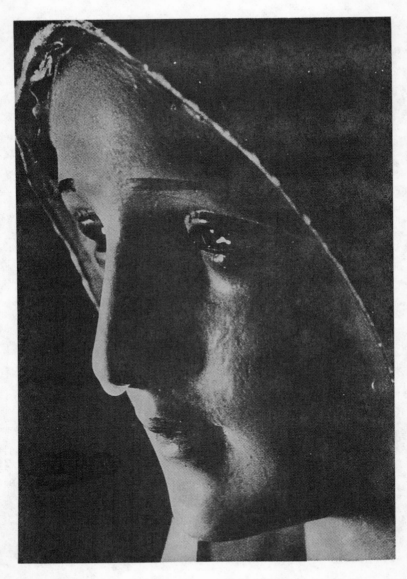

Photograph of the first Statue shedding tears in New Orleans, July 1972.

Padre Pio kisses the first Pilgrim Virgin statue, August 5, 1959, at San Giovanni Rotundo, Italy, as doves perch at Our Lady's feet.

In procession in Italy in 1959, doves again perch at Our Lady's feet.

Cardinal Gracias (Bombay, India) crowns the Virgin on pilgrimage in 1978 as Mr. Kaczmarek (left) looks on.

Fr. Matthew J. Strumski and Mr. Kaczmarek hold the wire-outline of the Pilgrim Virgin before the Black Madonna in Czestochowa, Poland, May 7, 1978. The inscription means: "Our Mother never leaves us."

Cardinal Sin of the Philippines assists in the deplaning of the Statue on December 5, 1985.

On pilgrimage to Springfield, Illinois in the Fall of 1980, Mr. Kacz-marek is interviewed on television outside the cathedral.

In Dallas, September 30, 1984, Mr. Kaczmarek leads a rally in honor of the Virgin.

Our Lady is for everyone. Mr. Kaczmarek presents her to elementary school students in Providence, Rhode Island.

The lighter side: Young Blue Army members welcome the Pilgrim
Virgin and Mr. Kaczmarek (who loves coffee) to Springfield, Massachusetts. The sign had originally been hung in the Hartford, Con-
necticut airport.

Mr. Kaczmarek and the Pilgrim Virgin statue in Springfield, Massachusetts.

Appendix A:
Interesting Rosary Statistics and Facts

Christ made the apostles "fishers of men" (Mark 1:17). He told them on one occasion to cast their nets on the right side of the boat after fishing all night without a catch (John 21:6) and they caught 153 fish (John 21:11).

In a complete Rosary there are 153 Hail Marys. In the Hail Mary there are, using the modern version of "you" for "thou", 153 letters. From May 13, the first apparition, to October 13, there are exactly 153 days.

Whatever the meaning of such numerical repetitions, we do know that at Fatima the Queen of Peace asked for the recitation of the Holy Rosary in every apparition:

May 13:	"Say the Rosary every day to obtain peace for the world."
June 13:	"I want you to say the Rosary every day."
July 13:	"I want you to continue to say the Rosary every day in honor of Our Lady of the Rosary."
Aug. 15:	"I want you to continue to say the Rosary every day in honor of Our Lady of the Rosary."
Sept. 13:	"Continue to say the Rosary."
Oct. 13:	"I want to tell you that I am Our Lady of the Rosary; continue to say the Rosary every day." [1]

Appendix B:
The Rosary Promises

The following is a summary of the promises made by Our Lady to St. Dominic, to whom the Rosary was first given, and to Blessed Alan, the Dominican Friar who did so much to spread the devotion in the fifteenth century:

1. To those who recite my Rosary devoutly, I promise my special protection.

2. To those who perseveringly say the Rosary, I will reserve some very special grace.

3. The Rosary shall be like strong armour against Hell; it will destroy vice and rout heresy.

4. The Rosary shall make virtue and good triumph; it shall substitute in hearts a love of God for love of the world and raise men's hearts to seek heaven.

5. Those who entrust themselves to me through the Rosary shall not perish.

6. Those who recite my Rosary with piety, meditating on the mysteries, shall not be overwhelmed with misfortune; neither shall they die a bad death.

7. Those truly devoted to my Rosary shall not die without the consolations of the Church.

8. Those who recite my Rosary shall find during their life and at the moment of death the light of God, the fullness of His grace and they will share in the merits of the blessed.

9. I will promptly deliver from Purgatory those souls who were devoted to my Rosary.

10. The true children of my Rosary shall enjoy great glory in heaven.

11. What you ask through my Rosary, you shall obtain.

12. Those who spread devotion to my Rosary shall receive from me aid in all their needs.

13. I have obtained from my Son the assurance that devotées of my Rosary shall have as their friends in life and in death the Saints of Heaven.

14. Those who recite my Rosary faithfully are my children—truly the brothers and sisters of my Son, Jesus Christ.

15. Devotion to my Rosary is a special sign of predilection.[2]

Appendix C:
The Scapular Promises

On July 16, 1251, Our Lady appeared to St. Simon Stock at Aylesford, England, holding in her hand the Brown Scapular of Mt. Carmel, saying to him,

> Receive, my beloved son, the Scapular of Thy Order, as the distinctive sign of my confraternity. Whoever dies invested with this Scapular shall be preserved from the eternal flames. It is a sign of salvation, a sure safeguard in danger, a pledge of peace and of my special protection until the end of the ages.[3]

The second traditional promise of Our Blessed Mother in favor of those who wear her Brown Scapular of Mt. Carmel is the Sabbatine Privilege made known to us through a Papal Bull issued March 3, 1322, by Pope John XXII, "On Saturday, as many as I shall find in Purgatory I shall free."[4]

To gain this privilege, one must : 1) Wear the Scapular faithfully after valid enrollment; 2) Keep chastity according to one's state; 3) Daily recite the Little Office of the Blessed Virgin or substitute a five decade Rosary with permission.

Mary's Motherhood is not limited to Catholics, it is extended to all men. Non-Catholics are encouraged to entrust themselves to Mary through her Scapular.

Appendix D:
Catholic Church's Endorsements
of the Fatima Apparitions

Jan. 17, 1918	The Diocese of Fatima is restored by Pope Benedict XV.
Oct. 13, 1921	The first Mass is celebrated in the Chapel of Apparitions in the Cova da Iria.
Oct. 13, 1930	The Bishop of Fatima declares the Fatima apparitions worthy of acceptance as of supernatural origin.
Oct. 31, 1942	Pope Pius XII consecrates the world to the Immaculate Heart of Mary.
May 4, 1944	Pope Pius XII institutes the Feast of the Immaculate Heart of Mary, on the twenty-fifth anniversary of the apparitions of Fatima.
May 13, 1946	Pope Pius XII crowns the image of Our Lady of Fatima and proclaims her "Queen of the World".
June 13, 1946	Pope Pius XII issues his encyclical "Deiparae Virginis Mariae", in which he refers favorably to Our Lady's message at Fatima.
Oct. 13, 1951	The Holy Year closing celebration takes place at the Marian shrine at Fatima.
July 7, 1952	Pope Pius XII consecrates the Russian people to the Immaculate Heart of Mary.
Oct. 11, 1954	In his encyclical "Ad Caeli Reginam" (establishing the feast of the Queenship of Mary) Pius XII refers to miraculous image of Our Lady of Fatima.
Nov. 12, 1954	The sanctuary shrine in Fatima is raised to basilica rank by Pope Pius XII.

Oct. 13, 1956	Pope Pius XII, through Papal Legate Eugene Cardinal Tisserant, blesses and dedicates the international headquarters of the Blue Army of Our Lady of Fatima, constructed near the shrine of Fatima.
Dec. 13, 1962	Pope John XXIII institutes the feast of Our Lady of the Rosary in honor of Our Lady of Fatima.
Nov. 21, 1964	Pope Paul VI renews Pius XII's consecration of Russia to the Immaculate Heart of Mary, speaking to the Fathers of the Second Vatican Council.
May 13, 1965	Paul VI sends a Golden Rose to Fatima confiding the "Entire Church" to Our Lady's protection.
May 13, 1967	Pope Paul VI goes to Fatima, where he calls for renewed consecration to the Immaculate Heart.
May 13, 1982	Pope John Paul II goes to Fatima to pray in thanksgiving for his surviving the attempted assassination on 5/13/81.

Appendix E:

Mary the dawn, Christ the perfect day;
Mary the gate, Christ the heavenly way.
Mary the root, Christ the mystic vine;
Mary the grape, Christ the sacred wine.
Mary the wheat, Christ the living bread;
Mary the stem, Christ the rose: blood-red.
Mary the font, Christ the cleansing flood;
Mary the chalice, Christ the saving blood.
Mary the temple, Christ the temple's Lord;
Mary the shrine, Christ the God adored.
Mary the beacon, Christ the haven's rest;
Mary the mirror, Christ the vision blest.
Mary the mother, Christ the Mother's Son;
By all things blest while endless ages run.

Anonymous

NOTES

[1]Rev. DeOca, Montes, c.c. Sp., *More about Fatima*, Philip Park Press, Manchester, England, p. 140.
[2]Rosarian Priests, *The Rosary Promises*, Ceylon.
[3]Carmelite Fathers, *The Scapular Apostolate*, 329 E. 28 ST., NYC, p. 6.
[4]*Ibid.*, p. 23.

Appendix F:

The *Boston Globe* of May 19th, 1986, carried an article with the caption "Philippines cardinal says Virgin Mary calmed crisis." The article by James L. Franklin went on to say:

> Cardinal Jaime L. Sin, who led the Catholic bishops of the Philippines in resistance to the dictatorship of Ferdinand Marcos, yesterday credited the nonviolence of his nation's revolution to the intervention of the Virgin Mary.
>
> Government troops, who held their fire when crowds blocked their advance on rebel forces, told him later that "a very beautiful lady appeared to them," Cardinal Sin said.
>
> The soldiers told him she said, "Stop. Don't attack my people, I am the queen of this land," the Cardinal said. . . .
>
> "I have not said this publicly before . . . ," said Cardinal Sin. "But I believed, in my heart of hearts, that there would indeed be a miracle and that our deliverance, when it comes, would come in peace, from the Lord, through his Mother's hands."

It was on November 19th, 1985, exactly six months earlier, that I was with the International Pilgrim Statue in the Boston Archdiocese when the phone call came from the office of Cardinal Sin requesting the statue in his land.